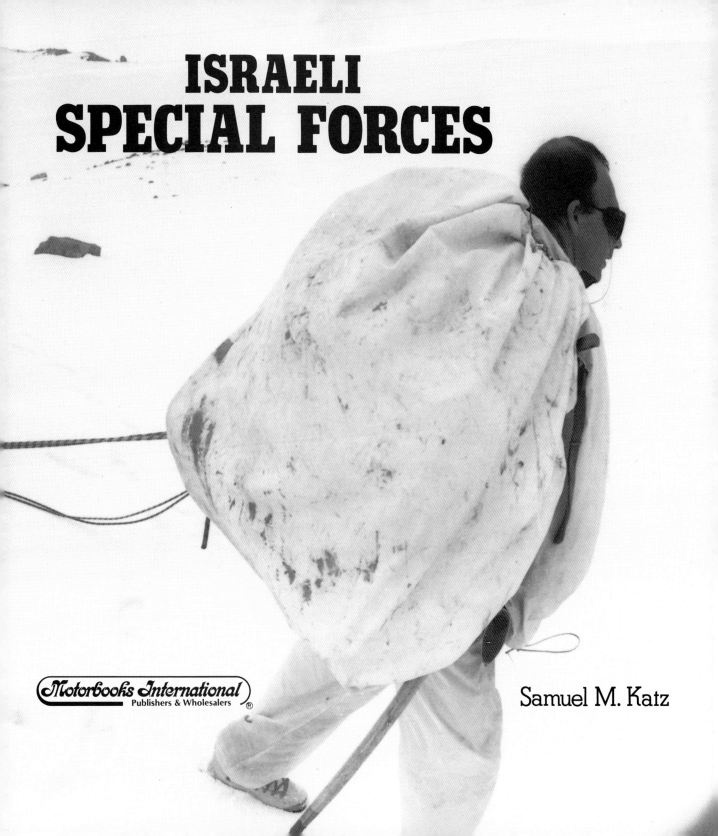

ISRAELI SPECIAL FORCES

Motorbooks International
Publishers & Wholesalers ®

Samuel M. Katz

First published in 1993 by Motorbooks International Publishers & Wholesalers, PO Box 2, 729 Prospect Avenue, Osceola, WI 54020 USA

Motorbooks International books are also available at discounts in bulk quantity for industrial or sales-promotional use. For details write to Special Sales Manager at the Publisher's address

Library of Congress Cataloging-in-Publication Data
Katz, Samuel M.
    Israeli special forces / Samuel Katz.
      p. cm.—(The Power series)
    Includes index.
    ISBN 0-87938-715-7
    1. Special forces (Military science)—Israel.
  I. Title.   II. Series: Power series (Osceola, Wis.)
  U262.K38   1993
  356′.167′095694—dc20   92-29758

On the front cover: Two Sayeret Giva'ati officers, wearing their distinctive purple berets and parachutist and Sayeret wings, enjoy a friendly moment before addressing their troops.

On the back cover: Upper left, a Sayeret Golani sergeant leads a fellow trooper through urban-combat training. Upper right, a Sayeret Giva'ati trooper emerges from a river to assault his target. Lower right, a Sayeret Giva'ati sniper sights through his scope. Lower left, Bedouin trackers search for clues that will lead them to terrorist infiltrators.

Printed and bound in Hong Kong

Contents

Preface

Over the past several years, a great deal of interest and fascination has focused on the term *special forces*. From the covert underwater operations of the U.S. Navy Sea, Air, and Land (SEAL) teams to the mysterious and secret operations of the British Special Air Service (SAS), commandos have captured the world's imagination with their spectacular feats and capabilities to accomplish the impossible. The term SEAL, for example, has come to personify a heavily camouflaged commando lurking in a flooded rice paddy in southeast Asia with an M-16 in one hand and a Gerber commando knife in the other; the very utterance of the word SAS conjures images of professional and dedicated warriors, adorned in black Nomex coveralls, storming an embassy building taken over by terrorists.

Israel's special forces, however, evoke no one specific image, no single or spectacular operation of grandeur, even though the Israel Defense Force's (IDF's) Chosen Units have been, it is easy to conclude, the world's busiest since 1945. They are an enigma. In fact, the operations, personality, and makeup of many of these units are so complex, so classified, and so shrouded in folklore that a complete history of Israel's combined commando forces and their operations is virtually impossible to compile in the space this format allows; unfortunately, several units, of both the past and the present, have had to be omitted. Because of the sensitive nature of many of the units examined in the following pages, many of the names of commanding officers and noncommissioned officers

(NCOs) are listed only by the first initials, or just by their first names. The purpose of this practice is to protect the identities of the personnel involved. Nevertheless, it is hoped that the following pages of this book and the photographs selected will offer a glimpse into the identity of these special warriors—who they are, what makes them unique, and what they are capable of doing on the field of battle.

The Israeli Ministry of Defense and the IDF spokesman are in no way connected to, nor have they participated in, the writing, production, or research of this book, and all opinions, reflections and conclusions belong solely to the author.

A book of this nature would not have been possible without the help and expertise of a great many people—many of whom, for obvious reasons of security, have requested to remain anonymous. I would like to thank Mr. Herzl Lavon at Israel Shipyards and Mr. Avi Goldbach at Israel Military Industries.

I offer special thanks to Lt. Col. Shai Dolev at the IDF Military Censor's Office for his office's quick and efficient review of this manuscript. Although many in the West, primarily in western Europe and North America, are uncomfortable with the dreaded *C*-word *censorship*, it is a necessity in a land like Israel, where the potential for war and terrorist attack exists on a permanent footing. It is imperative to stress that the IDF Military Censor's Office does not remove free thought, nor does it silence political criticisms; the only things removed by the censor's pen are military facts deemed too sensitive for national security to appear in print.

I in addition thank Mr. Nissim Elyakim for all of his logistical efforts on my behalf; this book would not have been possible without his direct assistance. Lastly, I thank my wife, Sigalit, for all of her love, understanding, and patience in seeing this project through.

All opinions and conclusions are my own.

Samuel M. Katz
May 1992

Introduction

H-3, Western Iraq, January 25, 1991

The first CH-53 chopper, adorned in a dull, almost invisible, muddy brown scheme and marked by the navy blue Star of David emblem, turned the landing strip at a secluded desert flatbed into a cyclone of sand and rock debris. The chopper didn't stay on the ground for long. It didn't need to. After its landing wheels hit the harsh desert floor, the aircraft, nicknamed the Yasur in the IDF's vernacular, opened its rear ramp, and a jeep armed with several FN MAG 7.62mm light machine guns raced out, as did over a dozen heavily armed reconnaissance paratroopers, loaded down with equipment and struggling with the weight of their burden to assume defensive firing positions. The exercise took less than 90 seconds, and before the CH-53 lifted off for a midair refueling rendezvous with an awaiting Israel Air Force (IAF) C-130 Hercules, the force of paratroopers, commanded and controlled by the jeep racing in the desert abyss, had spread out over a 200m perimeter to provide defensive cover for what would soon become a mini forward airfield.

The force commander, standing upright in his jeep and clutching an AK-47 assault rifle once owned by a Palestinian terrorist, held the receiver from his field radio and ordered in the troops. A few minutes later, a line of several C-130 Hercules transports—carrying reconnaissance paratroopers from Sayeret Tzanhanim (Paratroop Recon) reconnaissance infantry commandos from the Golani and Giva'ati Infantry Brigades, and reconnaissance troopers expert in hunting enemy tanks and in racing through the desert in jeep or on foot—were coming in for a landing. It was a risky undertaking to despatch the best of Israel's military elite deep into enemy territory, but Israel had no choice. It was the eighth day of Operation Desert Storm. Over a dozen Iraqi SCUD missiles had hit Tel Aviv and Haifa, and the reign of destruction had to end.

H-3, in this case, was a plateau in Israel's Negev Desert, and the planned raid, the opening attack of a full-scale Israeli commando offensive into Iraq, never materialized. The forces did train for such an eventuality, and such a plan, according to foreign reports, was to be used by the IDF Operations Branch to neutralize the portion of Iraq that Saddam Hussein had used as a launching pad for his unprovoked SCUD attacks. Perhaps political considerations had something to do with Israel's inaction—perhaps other, more delicate reasons the public is never meant to uncover. In any event, Sayeret Tzanhanim, the reconnaissance commando entity from the conscript paratroop brigade, was destined to play a deciding role in any IDF action taken against Iraq.

Nablus, the West Bank, November 11, 1991

During a routine tour of the area, Defense Minister Moshe Arens of Israel, a hard-line, right-wing, no-nonsense figure who passionately pursued Israel's national security, was visiting the "territories," along with several Defense Ministry officials, top-ranking IDF generals, and an entourage of Shin Bet (General Security Service) security men. Nablus is one of the hotbeds of the Intifadah, the five-year-long Palestinian uprising against Israeli rule. Terrorist activity, including the use of explosives and automatic weapons, has turned the teeming age-old city into a desperate battle zone. Through the ancient streets of the main market place, the local Palestinians looked on in stone-angry silence as the Defense Minister's retinue passed through the mysterious Casbah. The security contingent gazed nervously at the locals, up at rooftops (with sniper rifles), as well as inside darkened alleyways, always wary that an armed individual, willing to propel the plight of the Palestinians into the forefront of media attention, might actually make a deadly move.

No violence occurred that chilly winter's day, but a heavily armed "Palestinian" was in the crowd. Wearing a Jordanian-sewn blazer from a tailor shop in Amman, covered by a red and white Kefiyeh headdress, and clutching a tattered copy of an Arab-language newspaper, the young man carefully observed Defense Minister Arens' procession and hoped that he wouldn't get shot by accident. After all, he was carrying an Israel Military Industries Mini-Uzi 9mm submachine gun inside a leather holster and had a Beretta 9mm pistol strapped to his ankle. He was, of course, an undercover Israeli soldier, a paratrooper, a combat veteran, and a member of the elite Mista'aravim, or Arabists, undercover commando unit tasked with hitting the terrorist cells inside the West Bank and Gaza Strip hard and with stealth, speed, and the incredible Israeli gift of Chutzpah. He was a malignant presence in a sea of terrorists, and he had to maintain his cover at all times. Anything less would be certain death.

Needless to say, the disclosure that an IDF undercover commando, heavily armed no less, had come so close to Defense Minister Arens without the security detail receiving advanced word caused something of a major ruckus. The Defense Ministry wasn't pleased, and neither was the Shin Bet, which didn't fancy waging gun battles with its own in the center of a Palestinian town. Nevertheless, the incident, which received wide-spread coverage in Israel's notoriously independent newspapers, underscored what many Israelis had known for years: Terrorists, beware; our guys are the best, and they are out there among you.

Al-Na'ameh, Lebanon, Off the Coast of Damur, December 8–9, 1988

The two terrorists walking their posts inside the perimeter at the Popular Front for the Liberation of Palestine General Command's (PFLP-GC's) large base 20km south of Beirut were not expecting trouble that frigid winter's night, and they had slung their AK-47s around their shoulders during their tedious patrol of the organization's most important Lebanese base of operations. The silence that engulfed the entire mountainous region was a good sign that no Israeli air attack would come that night—but a strike did not necessarily have to come from the sky. Bleeding out of a concentration of foliage and large boulders were two thin, bright red laser beams, reaching across an 18m stretch and directly onto the chests of the two terrorists. At 0130 hours, commandos from Sayeret Golani, the reconnaissance force of the 1st Golani Infantry Brigade, aimed those thin bursts of laser light onto their targets and fired their silenced weapons, killing both Arabs and signaling the commencement of the commando raid. The operation's objective: the assassination of the PFLP-GC commander, Ahmed Jibril.

As far as conventional targets were concerned, al-Na'ameh was considered impregnable. It was protected by over 100 well-trained terrorists, and much of its nerve center was situated underground in bunkers reinforced by impervious blankets of steel, in Vietnamese-designed tunnels and natural caves. It was also the kind of "mission impossible" assignment the IDF General Staff usually delegated to Sayeret Golani, the IDF's premier conventional commando force.

The battle for al-Na'ameh lived up to all of its diabolical predictions. The firefights, waged in pitch-darkness, were close quarter, and much of the fighting was hand-to-hand; the Sayeret Golani commandos were equipped with a wide assortment of exotic equipment designed to turn night into day, including infrared goggles, laser sighting devices, and high-beam scopes. Foreign sources reported that the Golani commandos even brought in a dozen or so kamikaze dogs, Dobermans equipped with booby-trapped packs fitted with tear gas and C-4 explosives, to destroy the terrorists' underground bunkers and caves.

The Golani commandos were at al-Na'ameh for nearly 13 hours; the operation ended following a dramatic heliborne rescue of four stranded commandos from an encroaching guantlet of incredible terrorist fire. The final toll was over thirty terrorists killed and much of the base destroyed. In tragic, though all-too-typical fashion, the lone IDF casualty was a task force commander, Lt. Col. Amir Meital, who, like all Israeli special forces officers, had led from the front with an assault rifle in one hand and the words "Follow me" leaving his lips.

The raid at al-Na'ameh, a spectacular IDF operation, did fail in achieving its ultimate objective of killing—or, possibly, kidnapping—Ahmed Jibril. Nevertheless, the epic commando strike into the heart of enemy territory was a primer of Israel's national resolve to rid its borders of a terrorist presence. It was a classic commando operation and a classic Israeli example of military expertise. In essence, it was a microcosm of the IDF's historic reliance on commandos and elite reconnaissance formations as a preemptive first line of defense against enemies who outnumber and surround the Jewish State.

Israel's numerous elite forces, reconnaissance units, and commando formations have been *the* decisive equalizer in the six major wars and forty-four years of incessant bloodshed that have plagued the Arab-Israeli conflict. This is their story.

Chapter 1

The Founding Fathers: A Brief History

Under the guidelines of purist military thought, specially trained small units are a footnote to the pursuit of covert military operations during the gray areas of peacetime. During wartime, they are to be the cutting-edge attack force meant to hit hard deep behind enemy lines with explosive impact. Although every army in the world today deploys commandos for special operations, these soldiers are on the whole a luxury to be used for very specific contingencies. Israel, however, has

A Sayeret Golani sniper, calmly carrying his M-21 rifle, marches through the night en route to an engagement near the Lebanese border.

"The Old Man," Yitzhak Sadeh, the father of the Haganah's special forces, the Pal'mach, and virtually every other Israeli elite unit.

11

A new group of commissioned paratroop and Sayeret officers stand at attention as their new rank of second lieutenant will be unveiled for the first time. The courage and leadership capabilities of the IDF's special forces officer are legendary.

During the vicious battles for the hills surrounding Jerusalem, a Pal'mach sniper team engages the Arab Legion head-on. In the 1948 War of Independence, the Pal'mach was Israel's sole elite division-size entity.

never enjoyed the pleasure of selecting its enemies or the time when its national security is in dire jeopardy. Israel has been forced to use its elite forces, the most capable individuals in the nation's inventory, as raiders, reconnoiterers, and counter-terrorists virtually twenty-four hours a day, seven days a week, for the past forty-five years.

The elite forces of the Tzava Haganah Le'Yisrael, or IDF, have been forced into some of the most hellish conventional battles fought since the end of the Second World War and charged with achieving impossible missions thousands of kilometers from Israel's boundaries against a whole host of enemies—from rescuing hostages in the heart of central Africa to assassinating the heads of terrorist organizations in Beirut. Their ability to mount such long-range operations has transformed the Israeli military into a regional superpower. Their example has turned the IDF into a force of deterrence. The Chosen Units, as they are called in the IDF's unique vernacular, have become an imposing entity that the enemies of Israel have come to fear greatly.

Few nations on the face of this earth have been forced to rely on the courage, skill, and training of their commandos as completely as the State of Israel—from the first watchmen of nearly 100 years ago who dressed as Bedouins to the modern-day commando equipped with miniaturized communications gear and laser aim sights. Beginning with the first Zionist settlers to Palestine in the early twentieth century, the Jewish military visionaries realized that they were an underarmed and outnumbered entity in an extremely hostile and precarious region. The Jews could never hope to outgun the Arabs, but they could outfight them with great skill, unchallenged determination, and brilliant ingenuity. They *had* to be better fighters—plain and simple—to survive.

The first "elite" Jewish fighting unit was Ha'Shomer, or the Watchman, a defensive force of equestrians, sharpshooters, and hand-to-hand warriors tasked with protecting the first agricultural settlements of Jewish Palestine from marauding attacks by roaming Arab gangs. The unit was small but managed to make every round count and could hold off an enemy ten times larger. The men and women of Ha'Shomer began a tradition of few against many, of quality over quantity, and of egalitarian ideals in a universal responsibility for national defense.

Following the British Mandate over Palestine in 1919 and the creation of the Haganah, or Defense, the underground Jewish army in Palestine, the apparent need for a special military force appeared to have evaporated. Both the Arabs and the Jews were happy to see the Turks gone, and the British army, the mightiest military force in the colonial world, would be able to keep the precarious peace anywhere, even in Palestine. Then, in 1929, the Arabs rioted against the growing Jewish presence in Palestine. Bloodshed ensued, and hundreds of Jews were killed. The Haganah had no response.

In 1936, the Arabs rioted once again. This time, their offensive was not isolated to small Jewish enclaves, but engulfed the entire nation. The British army, like the Haganah, initially had no response, and eventually sanctioned the formation of the Notrim, or Guards, a special elite police force tasked with protecting isolated Jewish agricultural settlements.

Beyond being the first Jewish force trained in conventional fighting with conventional arms, the Notrim was, according to one former Israeli special operations officer, "the elite SWAT team of its day." Most important, the Notrim's potential for being the nucleus of a developing Jewish army attracted the likes of the elite young people of Jewish Palestine, including Yigal Allon, a future defense minister and general, and Moshe Dayan, one of Israel's most famous soldiers; they were all native-born Sabras with superb physical potential and the infrangible spirit of individuals with supreme military ambitions. (The word *Sabra* is Hebrew for a desert cactus fruit that, like its native-born Israeli namesakes, is hard and thorny on the outside, and soft and sweet on the inside.)

Three of Israel's most influential special operations officers, circa 1955: Unit 101 commander Ariel ("Arik") Sharon, standing, second from left; Sayeret Tzanhanim founder Meir Har-Zion, standing, far left; and the man who, as paratroop commander, chief paratroop and infantry officer, and chief of staff, deployed Israel's special forces more than anyone else in Israeli military history, Rafael ("Raful") Eitan, kneeling, far right.

With grenade in hand, a squad gunner from Sayeret Golani trains in assaulting fortified positions in the weeks prior to the outbreak of the 1967 Six Day War.

13

The Notrim's overall inability to crush the Arab riots attracted the attention of one Yitzhak Sadeh. Sadeh was a Crimean-born firebrand whose burly physical stature and innovative style of command had made him an influential Haganah officer. Determined to transform the "defensive" Haganah and the Notrim into a decisive and hard-hitting offensive element, he created a force of police-commandos whose principal weapons were mobility and the art of the night ambush; they were known as the Nodedot (Wanderers). The commandos of the Nodedot, subjected to brutal training and intensive indoctrination, never numbered more than seventy and possessed few rifles and pistols, but they managed to raid Arab villages harboring guerrillas at night—long before infrared equipment became standard issue.

In 1937, Sadeh enhanced the notion of elite mobile shock units, and the Plugot Sadeh, or Field Companies, were created. As would become standard practice for virtually every IDF elite unit, each Field Company commando was hand-picked by Sadeh and was forced to undergo a grueling preliminary examination before being allowed to volunteer into this secretive force. The most important qualities sought for entrance into the Field Companies were dedication and comradeship; the unit was a team more than anything else.

Another influential individual to enter the scene and who would have a lasting impact on the nature of the future IDF elite units was a young and highly eccentric British officer, Capt. Orde Charles Wingate. An expert in counterinsurgency tactics from his days in the Sudan, Wingate was

Sayeret Giva'ati soldiers gingerly walk through a beach after a landing exercise in southern Israel.

despatched to Palestine by the British High Command in 1936 to supervise the defense of the strategic oil pipelines originating in Iraq from marauding Arab terrorists. To achieve this objective, the zealous and Bible-thumping British army officer enlisted the support of the Jewish fighters, especially the young idealistic people from the Kibbutzim, or communal agricultural settlements; his real objective, many would argue, was to create the foundations for an elite Army of Zion, and he was to be its Gentile commander. Since the British had the expertise and weapons, and the Jews had the personnel and natural motivation, Wingate found a marriage of inconvenience between the two and formed the Special Night Squads (SNS), a small, though lethal, counterterrorist force that would bring the fight deep into the heart of enemy territory. Under Wingate, the Jews would no longer cower behind defensive emplacements. Defense meant offensive action, and striking deep into the heart of the enemy's territory with a rifle in one hand and a bayonet in the other. The Israeli reconnaissance commando was born.

Wingate, however, didn't last long in Palestine. His pro-Zionist disposition led the British to consider him a "security risk." His departure did not end the Haganah's newfound fascination with the prospects of elite forces. They would be needed.

When World War II erupted, the Haganah found itself in a terrible dilemma as Adolf Hitler's Final Solution of European Jewry loomed near. The British, with their infamous 1939 White Paper on Jewish immigration to Palestine, had cut off all Jewish immigration to Palestine at the time it was needed most. But the Haganah could not combat the British through military means when the war with Hitler, a true test of survival for the Jewish people, was in its initial stages. Initially, the British found little use for any Jewish military involve-

While pursuing Palestinian terrorists in the Jordan Valley during the 1967–70 War of Attrition, commandos from Sayeret Haruv, Central Command's reconnaissance unit, carefully advance toward a cave.

Naval commandos practice storming an enemy beachhead before assaulting a position along the Egyptian frontier in the War of Attrition.

Commandos from Sayeret Tzanhanim negotiate the muddy terrain of the Jordan Valley during a winter pursuit of a Palestinian terrorist.

ment, but that, too, would change. As German military success pushed the British deeper into the inner sanctums of the empire, especially into the Middle East and North Africa, and the Palestinian Arabs openly sided with the Nazis, the British were forced to resort to their only reliable ally in the entire region: the Jews. Once again, the British had the expertise and weaponry, the Jews possessed the personnel and motivation. On May 14, 1941, the Plugot Machatz (Pal'mach), or Strike Companies, was born.

In retrospect, the Pal'mach would be the most important influence in forging the tradition, success, and history of elite unit strategy into Israeli military doctrine. The Pal'mach was destined to be a fifth-column guerrilla force, an army of com-

In the IDF's true egalitarian tradition, a sharpshooter instructor makes sure that this class of Sayeret hopefuls will hit their target, square in the center, when they are deep behind enemy lines.

mandos and saboteurs that would conduct deep-penetration intelligence-gathering forays against enemy positions; it centered around a dedicated cadre of Field Company and SNS veterans. Yet the Pal'mach was much more than a test for small unit operations by a people without a country or army of its own. It would be an example for every other Israeli unit to follow. Its members were trained as

Two FN MAG gunners from a Sayeret Tzanhanim team enjoy a brief smile as they see the results of the sharpshooting on the firing line in northern Israel.

A Sayeret Golani grenadier aims his CAR-15/M203 toward a target, a row of empty fuel drums, during exercises atop the Golan Heights.

Sayeret Tzanhanim trainees, including an RPG grenadier, display their ability to hit the ground and roll over into firing position during their grueling basic training in central Israel.

17

An officer from Sayeret Ha'Druzim, a lesser known, though uniquely Israeli, special operations force, displays his "from-the-hip" marksmanship at a field firing range in northern Israel.

spies and demolitions experts, underwater swimmers, and cold-killers.

Although the British originally sanctioned the training of 1,000 Pal'mach fighters, the Haganah, realizing that this was a golden opportunity to form the nucleus of a professional and capable military elite, ingeniously fixed it so that over 3,000 fighters received instruction in the art of commando warfare. They were first used by the Allies in the invasion of Vichy Lebanon and Syria, where Pal'mach scouts were in the vanguard, clearing a path for advance and sabotaging key French defenses. The Pal'mach's operations earned it respect from all the Allied commanders, especially the Australians, who, according to Yigal Allon, liked the "Jews' cockiness" on the field of battle.

The Pal'mach was the first Israeli laboratory for creating specialized commando forces with extremely specific objectives. The Arab Platoon, a mixed force of Arabic-speaking natives, waged a

Reconnaissance paratroopers, carrying gas masks, practice for special operations in the desert prior to the outbreak of Operation Desert Storm and the 1991 Persian Gulf War.

guerrilla campaign against Axis targets in Syria and Lebanon and against Axis-controlled espionage cells in Jordan; when the Jewish State was to declare its independence, these fighters were to infiltrate behind Arab lines and monitor Axis troop movements.

The Pal'mach German Platoon was made up of German and Austrian refugees who, remarkably, were taught to become German Wehrmacht and SS soldiers so that they could infiltrate behind German lines as fifth-columnists should the Wehrmacht have succeeded in invading Egypt and then pushed on into Palestine. When the German advance was halted at el-Alamein, the German Platoon commandos were used as intelligence and rogue warriors: they infiltrated prisoner of war (POW) camps to gather intelligence, and operated with Capt. David Stirling's infamous Long Range Desert Group in the rolling sands of the North African desert; they were also destined to mount a raid against Erwin Rommel's desert headquarters.

The Pal'mach Balkan Platoon operated with the British SAS in the Aegean Sea, and the Romanian Platoon, tasked with sabotaging the ultrastrategic Ploesti oil fields, was rumored to have existed.

The motto was that the ultimate Pal'mach was a soldier with a weapon. Indeed, the Pal'mach fighter was trained to be proficient with every weapon to be found in the region—from a German

Purple Beret reconnaissance soldiers from Sayeret Giva'ati lay down some covering machine gun fire for a squad of tanks, uparmored Ma'Ga'Ch-7 Pattons, during large-scale maneuvers in the Negev Desert.

19

MP38 submachine gun to a British .303cal Lee Enfield rifle and a French Chatellerault 7.5mm light machine gun.

When World War II ended, so, too, did the marriage between the Pal'mach and the British, as the true battle for Israel's independence began. The Pal'mach's three brigades led the armed struggle by attacking British radar and police installations as well as battling the various Palestinian Arab forces for control of strategic areas. When the United Nations partitioned Palestine into both Jewish and Arab states, the Pal'mach mobilized its forces for full-scale war.

During the 1948 War of Independence, Pal'mach units took to the offensive when the outnumbered fighters in the newly formed IDF could barely maintain a defensive footing on the various embattled fronts. In the Negev Desert, in the Galilee, and amid the hard-fought rubble of the holy city of Jerusalem, determined Pal'mach units put together 10kg of homemade high explosives worth more than a battalion of soldiers and reinforced the familiar Pal'mach adage that the ultimate Pal'mach unit was a soldier with a weapon.

When the war ended in 1949, the Pal'mach was disbanded owing to the fear of its eventually becoming a militarily trained political elite, mainly because of the extreme and varied political views shared by many of the Pal'mach fighters. Nevertheless, by inventing the "Follow me" self-sacrificing ethic of command for its officers, the Pal'mach will go down in Israeli history as the IDF's first true military elite.

With the Pal'mach gone, the IDF was robbed of a living example that its other units could hope to emulate. Even though a paratroop battalion was formed in 1949, its members proved to be highly ineffective combatants with little stomach for special operations; in fact, the unit spent much of its time locating paratroopers moonlighting at local shipyards and attending funerals of comrades killed in freak training accidents.

The military balance between the Arabs and Israelis in the early 1950s wasn't as much a challenge to see which force would seize the initiative as it was to see which army would perform worse on the battlefield. The military malaise was forever changed in 1953 when the IDF ordered the formation of a small counterguerrilla force to stop Arab infiltrators. The group, which became known as Unit 101, and its commander, Maj. Ariel ("Arik") Sharon, would leave a lasting

During joint services with the Armored Corps, a Sayeret Tzanhanim grenadier force deploys from the rear section of a Merkava Mk. II main battle tank.

20

mark on every IDF elite unit that followed—even though it existed for only a little over six months.

Unit 101 took many of its tactics and combat ethics and much of its behavior from the Pal'mach—including striking at night, striking in small numbers, and attacking deep into enemy territory. Although Major Sharon enjoyed a friendly relationship with his fighters, who regarded him as one of their own rather than a commander, the Unit 101 soldiers performed in a highly disciplined fashion on the battlefield. They marched hundreds of kilometers into the enemy's unknown and never returned to base unless their mission was carried out successfully. Unit 101 also created the IDF's most infamous soldier, a scout named Lt. Meir Har-Zion, whose inherent combat and tracking skills were legendary and who was the only person in Israeli military history ever to be commissioned an officer without stepping foot inside the IDF's Officer School.

Although Unit 101 raids inside Jordan and Egypt virtually ended Arab infiltration into Israel within six months, the IDF General Staff decided to join the rabble-hearted commandos of the group with the fledgling 890th Battalion's paratroopers into a paratroop brigade named Unit 202. As always, the personality of officers such as Lieutenant Har-Zion, commander of the brigade's elite reconnaissance battalion, or Sayeret, would shape the IDF's image, as well as the entire Arab-Israeli battlefield, for years to come.

For the next forty years, the IDF emulated, expanded, and perfected the example of the Pal'mach and the brilliant, though brutal, success of Unit 101. The one lesson learned through the fifty years of having a small contingent of elite commandos set the stage for the rest of the nation's military entities was to create and foster many *specialized* units. For counterinsurgency work, the IDF created three territorial reconnaissance units of qualified paratroopers to safeguard a segment of the precarious borders with Egypt, Jordan, Syria, and Lebanon. These units were Sayeret Shaked, or Almond Recon, Southern Command's force; Sayeret Haruv, or Carob Recon, Central Command's recon force; and Sayeret Egoz, or Walnut Recon, Northern Command's force. The IDF Navy's Ha'Kommando Ha'Yami, or Naval Com-

mandos, was created from a dedicated corps of Pal'mach veterans and tasked with special amphibious operations.

Even the IDF's conventional elite units, its crack paratroop and infantry groups, were supplemented with their own commando forces. Sayeret Golani was the 1st Golani Brigade's reconnaissance force specialized in attacking Syrian positions atop the Golan Heights. Sayeret Tzanhanim, the paratroop brigade's reconnaissance element, inherited the mantle of Unit 101's legacy as a counterinsurgency, deep-penetration commando force uninhibited with any military predicament no matter who the enemy. And, in 1957, Sayeret Mat'kal, or General Staff Recon, was quietly formed as an ultra–top-secret, rogue force of intelligence-gathering warriors. In the years to

On April 1, 1991, at the Kirya in Tel Aviv, Lt. Gen. Ehud Barak, center, Israel's most decorated soldier and a commando genius who transformed the top-secret Sayeret Mat'kal into the world's finest special operations and antiterrorist unit, is appointed the IDF's fourteenth chief of staff.

follow, even more units, top-secret in nature, were made up of several dozen commandos each.

In the four major wars that have been fought since the creation of Unit 101, Israel's special forces have played an integral role in deciding the course of the conflicts—from the desert abyss of Sinai; to a guantlet of Syrian fortifications in the 1967 Six Day War; to the tarmac of Beirut International Airport and the frigid, inhospitable terrain of Fatahland near the Syria frontier during the 1967–70 1,000 Days War of Attrition; to the steep terror of Mt. Hermon and the torrid depths of the Red Sea during the 1973 Yom Kippur War. In between have been forays to Beirut (several), Entebbe, Tunis, the occupied territories, and, of course, southern Lebanon.

It can be argued that Israel's special forces have been responsible for the creation of the Jewish State, and they have certainly been responsible for its survival ever since. From independence to the present, they have executed some of the most difficult and dangerous commando strikes in modern military history and have become an entity much of the world holds in awe and that their enemies have come to fear with foreboding and doom.

The newest addition to the IDF's special operations equation, the McDonnell-Douglas AH-64 Apache, no doubt an airborne artillery platform to be used in support of Israel's various reconnaissance units behind enemy lines. Apaches were used in the March 1992 assassination of Hizbollah leader Sheikh Musawi in southern Lebanon.

Chapter 2

Sayeret Tzanhanim: Winged Snakes

Although they might be comrades-in-arms in the same brigade, a "regular" paratrooper is separated from a paratrooper in the Sayeret by tangible symbols, such as the Sayeret's small silver metal reconnaissance wings worn below the jump wings above the left breast pocket or the ex-"Arab" Soviet-produced AK-47 rifle carried as a personal weapon instead of the standard, though extremely lethal, Galil family of rifles. Emotional differences also separate the regular and reconnaissance Red Berets, such as the bonds that are forged with comrades in the seemingly endless months of basic training, where the impulses of the human spirit defeat a first lieutenant's efforts to break that spirit. Then, of course, on the field of battle are the other differences.

Winter in Lebanon is never enjoyable. With it come frigid, harsh winds; occasional blinding snow; and the type of climate that invites terrorists, be they Shi'ites in the Hizbollah (Party of God) movement looking to martyr themselves in the holy struggle to obliterate the Jewish State or a squad of well-trained and heavily armed Palestinians from the Popular Front intent on striking out against the Israeli frontier. The cold makes the Israeli soldiers, and their Christian allies in the South Lebanon Army (SLA), wary. It affects their judgment and ability to maintain a vigil against possible attack. Terrorists adore the bitter Lebanese winters. So, too, however, does Sayeret Tzanhanim.

The night of November 19, 1990, Capt. Yaron Yogav, a veteran Sayeret Tzanhanim officer who was typical of the young men of his generation, had led a squad of reconnaissance paratroopers into the devil's lair—across the Israeli border, past the 15km self-imposed security zone that Israel maintains with the SLA, and 6km deeper into southern Lebanon, in the Mt. Dov area. Their mission that ice-cold Lebanese night was to lay an ambush. This was nothing new for Captain Yogav

During a training exercise meant to simulate long-range-penetration probing actions in enemy territory, a force of Sayeret Tzanhanim commandos is provided with new supplies courtesy of the IAF.

and his troopers. They had taken this path count-less times before, and, according to one Sayeret Tzanhanim officer, "It was the type of operation they enjoyed." After all, Captain Yogav's subordinates were from a generation far different from that of Sayeret Tzanhanim's founders. These early "commandos" made their military service breakthroughs in the gray period of the Intifadah, where the rules of engagements were beset by muddled politics and close-quarter battles against youths wielding hatchets and hurling Molotov cocktails. To a unit like Sayeret Tzanhanim, trained to hit hard, hit fast, and hit permanently, removing the commandos from the police duty and day-to-day doldrums of the Palestinian uprising and taking them to the field for some training or an operational assignment was, a Sayeret Tzanhanim officer said, "like giving the paratroop recon commandos an aspirin; sending them to the Purple Line [officially, the Lebanese frontier] [was] like giving them an anti-Intifadah antibiotic." It helped them remove the edge, refocus their true mandate. Rest and relaxation techniques like these had their price, however.

Commandos from Lt. Meir Har-Zion's Sayeret Tzanhanim assemble following the successful execution of Operation Olive Branch, December 11, 1955, against Syrian gun emplacements at the base of the *Golan Heights. Some of the commandos carry weaponry and wear uniforms captured from their Syrian victims.*

Intelligence had predicted that a force of Shi'ite terrorists was planning to head into the security zone and then to the Israeli frontier. Captain Yogav's force was to stop them. The squad's journey had been a typical page out of the Sayeret Tzanhanim rule book. A formation of soldiers loaded down with dozens of kilos of equipment and ammunition, carrying their assault rifles with two magazines taped together for good measure, conducted a silent and stealthy forced march through inhospitable terrain. It was difficult to cross vast stretches of territory laced with rocks, boulders, and impassable foliage with speed

and in silence even in the daylight, but these were the fighters of Sayeret Tzanhanim. In the lengthy months of their training, they had learned to use their left and right legs as vehicles of nonstop movement and survival. At first, the distance was short, though brutal: 5, 10, and even 15 "klicks" at a time. During training, the commando wanna-be's learned to pace themselves until they reached their 120km terror, a rite of passage that must be breached, right before the end of their commando instruction.

Captain Yogav's men would not have to make 120km that night in November 1990, but their

Sayeret Tzanhanim's reconnaissance paratroopers are readied for a training jump in southern Israel in 1965.

With the exception of the Mitla Pass operation, the unit has never parachuted into an engagement.

challenge was, nevertheless, daunting. They were to lie in ambush, just south of the hotbed of Hizbollah power in the area: the village of Ein A'ta, in the eastern half of southern Lebanon. Lying in ambush is a difficult enough assignment for any soldier—let alone one who had earned a spot in the Sayeret. Hidden by the bush, forced to position one's weight atop body-piercing load-bearing equipment while the frigid and damp soil begins to seep into one's bones, causes the first occurrence of instant arthritis. It is not the best way to begin a lightning-fast military strike. An ambush was a cheap shot: a surprise assault where the target was not supposed to know what had hit it or where the assault had come from.

Captain Yogav had dispersed his squad in textbook fashion: two FN MAG 7.62mm light machine gunners, known as Magists, covered the approach to a thin dust road, and the area was covered by several riflemen, as well as an antitank gunner armed with a Soviet-produced RPG-7 antitank rocket and a couple of grenadiers mixed in for good measure. Foreign reports said the men were all equipped with night-fighting equipment, including laser sights and infrared goggles.

At a little after 0200 hours, Captain Yogav gazed across the sleepy landscape and discovered four bright beams of light bursting through his infrared field glasses. It was the headlights emanating from two cars, Japanese-made sedans—but

A Sayeret Tzanhanim team is briefed by its commander before setting out on a reconnaissance patrol *of the Egyptian frontier in the days prior to the outbreak of the 1967 War.*

this wasn't a main thoroughfare where rush-hour commuters headed home from jobs in the city. The only people out at that hour were those looking for a fight.

The cars were 100m away and were closing in fast. The orders were issued for his soldiers to prepare for battle. Weapons were held ever so much tighter, safeties removed, and final breaths of the frosty air inhaled before adrenaline would take over.

When the vehicles came to within 30m of the Sayeret Tzanhanim commandos lying in wait, Captain Yogav assumed the initiative and opened fire. Hundreds of red and green tracer rounds, followed by the flickering explosions of regular 5.56mm and 7.62mm fire, turned the Lebanese bush into a scene from *Star Wars*. The fusillade of automatic fire from the Sayeret Tzanhanim ambush position was devastating. It was meant to destroy both vehicles in seconds, before any terrorist could return fire, but Murphy's Law took over. Both cars were struck with a cataclysmic barrage, but one of the terrorists managed to emerge from the driver's seat and launch a burst of automatic fire in the direction of the flashing muzzle blasts. Captain Yogav, leading his commandos toward the two targeted vehicles a few yards ahead of his unit, was struck in the head and killed instantly. At the age of twenty-two, he was buried the following morning, on the day he was supposed to have been released from active duty. His self-sacrifice and penchant for commanding his legions at the helm, yelling, "Follow me," had, as their reward, cost the ultimate price.

Counterterrorist operations are not a Sayeret Tzanhanim trademark. They are, however, a form of warfare that the unit has had to learn through absolute necessity. Sayeret Tzanhanim's specialty is the type of operation that most enemies only find out about the morning after. But the ambush at point X on a battalion commander's map somewhere in the treacherous abyss of southern Lebanon was like many Sayeret Tzanhanim operations since the early 1950s. It was an effort deep behind enemy lines, carried out by a small force of highly trained, completely motivated commandos confident in their abilities as special forces soldiers and cohesion as a team and a unit. The

Sayeret Tzanhanim is a unit that operates in the mysterious "black" area of covert operations, and many of its missions are state secrets of the highest order.

Negotiating impassible and impossible terrain is one of the many talents that Sayeret Tzanhanim has, as shown by a force of soldiers climbing a deep desert embankment.

The first true commander of a conscript paratroop brigade's reconnaissance element was the ultimate Israeli commando: 1st Lt. Meir Har-Zion. The famed Unit 101 veteran was named Sayeret Tzanhanim commander in 1954. The "regular" Israeli paratroopers circa 1954 were a far cry from the paratroopers who today wear the red beret and the silver metal jump wings; the first Sayeret, when compared with the unit of today with its handheld antitank weapons and laser sights, was a small and primitive group of soldiers who were more trailblazers than anything else. Virtually every member of the first Sayeret Tzanhanim was a Unit 101 refugee who had found a brief home in the 890th Paratroop Battalion's elite Company D. They were all fighters who found the trappings of normal combat service abhorrent. They wanted to conduct their training marches in Jordanian or Egyptian territory. They wanted to be the unit the Israeli leadership called upon when retaliation was the order of the day—when a foray against an Egyptian military post, a Jordanian police station, or a Syrian gun emplacement was deemed necessary as a statement of national resolve that no other force could execute. They were also fighters who demanded to be in the vanguard of covert special operations, be they cross-border intelligence gathering or dirtier deeds of preemptive

Sayeret Tzanhanim commandos from Maj. Matan Vilnai's task force engage Palestinian terrorist positions at Karameh during Operation Hell, March 23, 1968.

violence (many of these operations are still classified). The soldiers of Sayeret Tzanhanim, all four dozen of them, demanded this unique role in Israeli military strategy for obvious reasons. They were the best soldiers Israel had in its small order of battle. They could run faster, march farther, and shoot straighter than any other unit. They trained incessantly and considered anything but the complete execution of a mission to be a total failure.

Sayeret Tzanhanim became an exclusive club, and to join its membership required a special type of soldier cut from a unique block of granite. The reconnaissance force was so small that few people outside the paratroopers' command structure knew of its existence. Conscripts could not simply volunteer into the Sayeret; they had to endure the rigors of service in the battalion, and later the brigade, before Lieutenant Har-Zion could observe them as regular Red Berets and then, if he determined that they displayed the special qualities required to become a reconnaissance commando, offered them the privilege of volunteering into the Sayeret. Even then, wishing to wear the reconnaissance wings meant nothing. Before Lieutenant Har-Zion would allow any reconnaissance hopeful to follow him behind enemy lines, the paratrooper needed to undergo a grueling physical, psychological, and emotional test period, where he was sure to be broken. If the hapless conscript was damaged beyond conceivable repair in the sadistic examination, he was offered a thumbs down and duly sent back to the battalion for the completion of his military service. If the trooper could pick himself up by the bootstraps and persevere, Har-Zion would formally accept him into the fold. Although the means for selecting and training Sayeret Tzanhanim commandos would change somewhat in the coming years, this was a proven method for ensuring that the paratroopers' best unit was, indeed, made up of Israel's finest soldiers.

Unit 101 was disbanded following its six months of explosive service because it became too politically volatile as a counterguerrilla force, but, oddly enough, Sayeret Tzanhanim would follow its mantle without respite. The Sayeret primarily launched small unit—one- or two-squad—attacks in response to Arab terrorist operations against

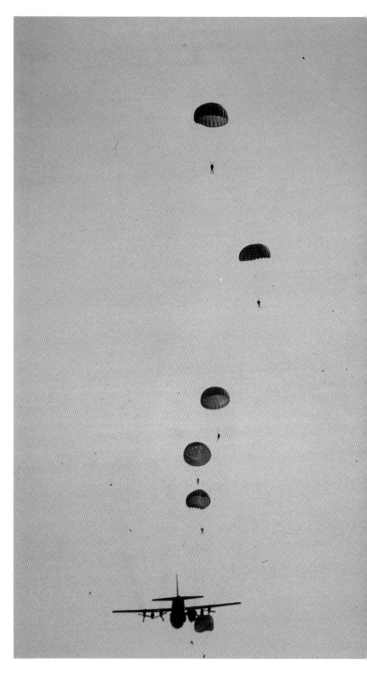

You have to jump to earn your wings. The long line of parachutes open beneath an IAF C-130 Hercules during Sayeret Tzanhanim jump training.

Israel. Several large-scale operations were initiated, however. One of the most symbolic of such operations where the Sayeret played an instrumental role, as well as served as the exemplary model for the remainder of the brigade, was Operation Olive Leaves. That December 11, 1955, retaliatory raid involved virtually the entire paratroop battalion and struck against a series of Syrian military fortifications on the eastern bank of the Sea of Galilee. The overall objective of the raid was to capture Syrian soldiers who could later be swapped for four Sayeret Tzanhanim commandos seized by the Syrians while conducting a top-secret intelligence-gathering mission atop the

Golan Heights one year earlier. The specific objective of the Sayeret that bone-chilling rainy evening was to assault a series of fortified Syrian pillboxes that several IDF operations officers had once labeled as impregnable.

Emerging from a banana field engulfed by a torrential downpour, Har-Zion's commandos assaulted the Syrian positions with guns ablaze. The fusillade was so fierce that many Syrian soldiers simply ran off wildly into the distance in unsuccessful attempts to evade the Sayeret's wrath. Before the Tzanhanim task force headed back to Israel, fifty-five Syrian soldiers had been killed, and a further twenty-nine captured; they were later

With their antennas bristling in the wind, Sayeret Tzanhanim commandos regroup during their assault on Egypt's Sedwan Island in Operation Rhodes, Janu- *ary 22, 1970, in the closing days of the War of Attrition. They all carry AK-47s captured from the Egyptian army.*

exchanged for the four Sayeret Tzanhanim captives held by Damascus.

From his countless operations behind enemy lines, it appeared as if Lieutenant Har-Zion was going to command Sayeret Tzanhanim forever. But this Israeli superman's mortality was uncovered by a Jordanian .303 bullet, fired by a sniper, during Operation Jonathan, the September 11, 1956, retaliatory counterterrorist raid against the Jordanian police fort at a-Rawha on the West Bank. A miraculous battlefield operation removed the bullet fragment from Har-Zion's throat, and his life was spared, but his career terminated. A true legend in the art of irregular warfare, a man who could navigate his way through a maze of enemy territory, had been humbled. Sayeret Tzanhanim's operations and place in Israeli military history were only just beginning.

On October 29, 1956, Capt. Rafael ("Raful") Eitan's 890th Paratroop Battalion parachuted into infamy at the Mitla Pass in the Sinai Peninsula, in the first spark of the 1956 Sinai Campaign. Sayeret Tzanhanim, the unit's reconnaissance force, was instrumental in the battalion's plans to seize the ultra-strategic pass so that the cream of Israel's armored might could race on to the Suez Canal unmolested. Although it wasn't the first paratroop unit to enter the Mitla Pass, Sayeret Tzanhanim played a role in this capture.

For the next ten years, the region remained relatively quiet—by Middle Eastern standards, that is. For Sayeret Tzanhanim, occasional retaliatory raids were mixed in with the constant regimen of combat training. By 1967, the unit had changed dramatically since its days under Meir Har-Zion. It was no longer a ragtag force of rogue warriors, but was now a disciplined force of conventional special forces soldiers, capable of waging commando strikes anywhere in the immediate region. Its commander was a young and charismatic officer named Dan Shomron, a future war hero and eventual IDF chief of staff.

When, on June 4, 1967, the Six Day War erupted, Sayeret Tzanhanim was assigned to Raful Eitan's paratroop brigade task force in Sinai, and it waged a mobile campaign of destruction against Egyptian armor formations. Although excellent close-quarter combatants, Major Shomron's recon-naissance soldiers assumed an antitank role, equipped with jeeps mounting 106mm recoilless rifles. During the battle of Firdan Bridge, at the gateway to the imposing waters of the Suez Canal, Major Shomron's commandos inflicted devastating damage on a mighty Egyptian armor force; dozens of brand-new Soviet-produced T-55 main battle tanks, right off the freighter in Alexandria harbor, were destroyed by the commandos' merciless fire. With the battle over, and the remnants of Egypt's armor might laying in smoldering ruin, the Sayeret Tzanhanim commandos parked their jeeps and washed their feet in the refreshing canal waters.

It was the role of Sayeret Tzanhanim in the 1,000 Days War of Attrition, a three-year war of shattered nerves that followed the end of the Six Day War, that proved to be the turning point for the soldiers who wear the dagger wings across their chests. It was a conflict of tit-for-tat, of Arab commando attack or terrorist infiltration that warranted an Israeli special forces response every time. It was the golden age of Israeli special operations. Sayeret Tzanhanim would leave its mark on the battlefield from the treacherous

Reconnaissance paratroopers are heli-lifted, courtesy of an IAF CH-53 Yasur, to the hellish close-quarter battles in the Ein el-Hilweh refugee camp near Sidon on the third day of Operation Peace for Galilee.

A Bell-212 chopper pops in to pick up a Sayeret Tzanhanim team from a Maidun hilltop. Close coordination between Sayeret Tzanhanim and the IAF is an intrinsic element of the unit's ability to mount special operations behind enemy lines.

confines of the Lebanese frontier to the Golan Heights, the Jordan Valley, and the Sinai Desert.

Hundreds of special forces operations were carried out, some minor, others simply awe inspiring. In the southern theater of operations, against Egypt, one famous Sayeret Tzanhanim campaign was the November 1, 1968, Operation Shock, a heliborne commando raid deep into the heartland of Egyptian Africa. In all, fourteen fighters, the elite of the elite unit, led by Maj. Matan Vilnai, commander of the Sayeret—a highly decorated commando officer who later attained the rank of major general and became commander of the IDF Southern Command—were ferried to an Egyptian powerplant in the Nile Valley at Naja'a-Hamadi by two French-built Sud.Aviation SA 321K Super Frelon choppers and proceeded to destroy the facility with a potent load of high explosives.

In the Jordan Valley, Sayeret Tzanhanim participated in countless pursuits of terrorists infiltrating across the Jordan River into the West Bank.

A Sayeret Tzanhanim officer, looking concerned and fatigued, stands over the body of a Palestinian terrorist killed as he attempted to move through the security zone in southern Lebanon and a paratrooper ambush.

The Mirdafim, as the pursuits became known, were brutal exercises in small unit cooperation and determination—following a terrorist squad's tracks in desert terrain under a 50 degree Celsius ovenlike sun. If the Sayeret Tzanhanim task force, usually a few noncommissioned officers (NCOs) commanded by an officer or two, failed to interdict the terrorists before they reached safety in a West Bank city, these individuals could perpetrate a major act of violence inside one of Israel's major cities. The commandos of Sayeret Tzanhanim, as well as other Sayeret operations in the Jordan Valley, viewed their day-to-day treacherous maneuvers as a race against time. Assaulting a desert cave where terrorists were held up took enormous courage and combat skill—many Sayeret officers and NCOs fell in battle.

During the campaign against the fledgling Palestinian terrorist forces based in Jordan, Sayeret Tzanhanim participated in the suitably named Operation Hell, the March 21, 1968, strike against the Jordanian town of Karameh. In Operation Hell, IDF armor, air, and regular paratroop units assaulted heavily fortified terrorist facilities, while the Sayeret, commanded by Major Vilnai, was helilifted into the surrounding mountains to cut off any terrorist retreat. In the north, along the Lebanese and Syrian frontiers and in the terrorist-infested Fatahland region near Mt. Hermon, Sayeret Tzanhanim participated in dozens of cross-

A Sayeret Tzanhanim FN MAG gunner stares nervously through the sights of his 7.62mm light machine gun as he sits inside the confines of a command car during a patrol of the Lebanese border on a bone-chilling winter's night.

border assaults where it launched daring commando strikes against terrorist positions as well as positions held by Syrian infantry soldiers and paratroopers.

Several spectacular Sayeret Tzanhanim operations were initiated against Palestinian terrorist positions throughout Lebanon—from the northern port city of Tripoli to the streets of downtown Beirut. On December 27, 1968, in retaliation for Lebanon's allowing Palestinian terrorists from Dr. George Habash's Popular Front for the Liberation of Palestine (PFLP) to use Beirut as a staging ground for deadly attacks against El Al Israel Airlines, a mixed task force of Sayeret Mat'kal and

Sayeret Tzanhanim commandos was heli-lifted to the sprawling Beirut International Airport and proceeded to destroy thirteen Lebanese airliners.

On February 20–21, 1973, in Operation Hood 54–55, Sayeret Tzanhanim participated in a multi-unit commando raid against Palestine Liberation Organization (PLO) and Black September training facilities in a series of refugee camps near Tripoli in the farthest operation ever until then mounted from Israel's shores.

On April 9, 1973, Sayeret Tzanhanim once again returned to Lebanon, as an invaluable segment of Operation Spring of Youth, a joint Mossad–IDF/Navy–Sayeret Mat'kal–Sayeret

With the smoke of a grenade evaporating into a cloud of cordite, two recon paratroopers race into a fortified room during maneuvers in Hell Town.

Tzanhanim raid against Black September's leadership and key logistics positions in downtown Beirut as well as in the coastal city of Sidon. During the raid, a force of Sayeret Tzanhanim commandos, camouflaged as hippies and tourists in civilian garb, attacked the headquarters of Nayif Hawatmeh's Democratic Front for the Liberation of Palestine (DFLP), a fanatic Palestinian group. The close-quarter and hand-to-hand fighting that followed was lethal. Dozens of terrorists were killed, as were two Sayeret Tzanhanim officers. The raid, however, came to personify much of what Sayeret Tzanhanim was all about: executing the unexpected.

When, on October 6, 1973, the armies of Egypt and Syria launched their surprise attack against Israeli positions on Yom Kippur Day, virtually every Israeli military formation, including Sayeret Tzanhanim, was caught by surprise. Sayeret Tzanhanim did not see itself exclusively deployed on any single front, although one operation, in a

In the middle of their basic training, a long way from wearing the Sayeret wings, a group of Sayeret Tzanhanim hopefuls clutch their Galil assault rifles as their unit commander lectures on the Sayeret's illustrious history.

Already having earned their coveted red berets, Sayeret Tzanhanim candidates await their jump instructor and their first experience with hurling themselves from an airplane, following the seemingly endless basic training.

desperate theater of operations, earned the unit permanent fame: it was known as Operation Nightgown. At 2300 hours on the foggy night of October 12, at the height of the fighting between Syrian and Israeli forces, a single IAF CH-53 Yasur chopper landed at a grassy opening near Kasr al-Hayr, on the main Baghdad-Damascus Highway approximately 100km from the Syrian capital. While a small force of paratroopers guarded the chopper, twelve paratroopers and a jeep fitted with a 106mm recoilless rifle headed out for a bridge where a brigade of Iraqi T-62 tanks was about to cross en route to the Golan Heights fighting. The Iraqis would never make it. As they approached the enemy troopers and tanks, the Sayeret Tzanhanim commandos and their jeep-mounted gun sprang into action, attacking from the front and causing a bottleneck. Trapped, the Iraqis fell prey to a murderous barrage of machine gun and grenade fire from the rear, where several other Israeli commandos armed with rocket-propelled grenades (RPGs) unleashed their destructive wrath. Other Sayeret Tzanhanim commandos placed explosive charges underneath the bridge full of burning vehicles. By the time the CH-53 chopper lifted off, the entire bridge had erupted into a fiery ball of devastation. Invaluable Iraqi reinforcements, crucial to the Golan fighting, never reached the front.

Operation Nightgown was one of the smallest Israeli special operations ever mounted, and also one of the most important. Sayeret Tzanhanim

Having survived the Gibush, having survived the conventional portion of paratrooper's basic training, Sayeret Tzanhanim hopefuls now attempt to live through the process that will earn them their jump wings.

also played an important role in the Israeli counterattack against the Egyptians, especially in the crossing of the Suez Canal and the bitter, close-quarter, hellish fight around Suez City.

Sayeret Tzanhanim's most famous action was its part in the July 3–4, 1976, Operation Thunderball rescue of Jewish and Israeli hostages from Entebbe Airport in Uganda. Although elements from Sayeret Mat'kal were tasked with the actual rescue of the 103 hostages, units from Sayeret Tzanhanim played a crucial role: they placed beacons alongside the runways to ensure that the armada of C-130s could take off in the pitch black night without hindrance. Sayeret Tzanhanim was also responsible for silencing the Ugandan Army's

presence at Entebbe and eliminating any hostile threat that may be posed to the hostages and the Israeli aircraft. Some of the fighting between the Sayeret Tzanhanim commandos and the Ugandan soldiers was fierce; many private, small hand-to-hand battles transpired. Although Operation Thunderball—later renamed Operation Yonatan in honor of Lt. Col. Yonatan ("Yoni") Netanyahu, the mission's commander—was a combined effort of a great many units, Sayeret Tzanhanim's role was perhaps the most important to its overall success.

Many of Sayeret Tzanhanim's activities in the subsequent years, including its participation in the June 6, 1982, Operation Peace for Galilee, are

Beret March—Sayeret Tzanhanim style! Carrying their "Mapatz" antitank missiles and launchers on their back, a force of Sayeret Tzanhanim trainees, with *the help of a Boombeat radio blaring Led Zeppelin's greatest hits, heads through kilometer number 80 on a 120km forced march.*

classified. The unit did, however, take part in one of the most brutal battles of the Lebanon war: the conquest of the Ein el-Hilweh refugee camp. Situated near the sprawling Mediterranean city of Sidon, Ein el-Hilweh was defended by fanatic elements of the Syrian-controlled Palestinian movements. They were determined to fight to the last person and, taking the camp's residents hostage in the process, willing to martyr several thousand innocent souls, as well. As a result, the Sayeret, supported by units from the parent brigade, was forced to storm each block, building, and room individually. The fighting was hellish, as it took days to assume control over a single street. Lesser units would not have been able to battle the dug-in guerrillas without suffering horrendous loss of life, but Sayeret Tzanhanim persevered and regrouped through incessant barrages of enemy fire.

Maidun and Operation Law and Order took place on May 4, 1988, a few weeks following Israel's fortieth anniversary. For months, the Shi'ite Hizbollah terrorist organization had been launching a multitude of terrorist attacks, attempting to inch ever so much closer to the Israeli frontier. About eighty Hizbollah gunmen had turned the small village of Maidun, situated strategically close to the Israeli border, into its base of operations. Every rooftop became an antiaircraft position, and the city's streets became fortified gauntlets of automatic and antitank fire. When Israel struck, it called upon its paratroopers—led, of course, by its Sayeret—to neutralize the village. Supported by a force of heavy armor, the paratroopers moved into Maidun ready for an epic battle. Sayeret Tzanhanim commandos entered the town in modified and rearmored American-produced M113 armored personnel carriers (APCs) and the IAF Bell-212 choppers, and cleared the village in the urban-warfare purification method they had trained incessantly to perfect. The Hizbollah fighters gave as good as they got, however, and dozens of hand-to-hand battles soon erupted, as did countless pointblank exchanges with RPGs and .50-caliber heavy machine guns. The fighting was so fierce that LAW rockets were also used at pointblank range. Hours after the first rounds of 5.56mm fire was launched and over fifty

Hizbollah gunmen lay dead, the paratroopers razed much of Maidun with over 500kg of high explosives. The cost to the Tzanhanim and its Sayeret was steep: two officers and an NCO were killed in the action, and dozens others seriously wounded.

So, what is it that propels an eighteen-year-old Israeli conscript, after all of 2 hours in an IDF uniform, to want to volunteer into Sayeret Tzanhanim—a demanding unit whose operations, covert and overt, are the most dangerous that can be mounted? Some, especially from the Kibbutzim and Moshavim, or cooperative settlements, volunteer because it's tradition. Their fathers were members of one Sayeret or another, their brothers were in a Sayeret or another one of Israel's special forces, and *all* of their friends and classmates intend to volunteer into one of the various IDF Sayerot; several will, no doubt, try out for pilot training, several for service in the naval commandos, and several to be airborne rescuers in the IAF's elite Aeromedical Evacuation Unit (AEU). In fact, these egalitarian eighteen year olds come to the IDF's Absorption and Assortment base, better known by its Hebrew acronym Basis Klita U'Miyun (Ba'Ku'M), on the first day of their military service equipped with all the proper essentials. They are all physically fit, they are all used to working as a team and within some larger framework, and most face enormous peer pressure to return home with a red beret, brown leather jump boots, and reconnaissance wings. If a soldier ends the brief stint in Ba'Ku'M as a trainee in a Sayeret, then the soldier has achieved a long-sought-after victory. If the soldier is refused a spot in the recon and is accepted as a volunteer in the regular conscript paratroop brigade, it is only "acceptable"; the same holds true for service in the Golani and Giva'ati Infantry Brigades, the Armored Corps, and the Combat Engineers.

Others arriving in Ba'Ku'M are astute students of history. They recall battles in Israel's past, and landmarks of courage and sacrifice: the Mitla Pass, Qantara, Karameh, the Jordan Valley, Beirut International Airport, Shedwan Island, Chinese Farm, Entebbe, and Ein el-Hilweh. Virtually every Israeli knows of the exploits of the regular paratroopers, their symbols, and their history. They have all heard of the motto Acharei Ha'Tzanhanim, or After the Paratroopers, and all know the honor and responsibility that come with the silver metal jump wings. They know that they want to be paratroopers and, yes, if possible, members of the elite Sayeret Tzanhanim club.

Then come those simply seeking acceptance into a rigid framework where they can prove themselves as men, as soldiers, and as human beings. They are what one experienced paratroop NCO temporarily stationed at Ba'Ku'M labels "Wanderers": conscripts with extraordinary potential simply searching for a home. They are endeared through the Ba'Ku'M process of being photographed, fingerprinted, and inoculated; issued a personal serial number, new uniforms reeking of starch, uncomfortable boots, dog tags,

and a kitbag; and then despatched into a "company" for their two-day to three-week stint at finding a home in the Army, Navy, or Air Force. Less than 24 hours into their 26,280 hours of conscripted service, these recruits are ushered around a series of tents, each of which represents a different branch of the IDF open to volunteers or willing to accommodate those really interested in joining their ranks. It is like recruitment week at a major university, although here the "head-hunters" carry CAR-15 and Glilon assault rifles and can offer only three years of solid guaranteed employment as a combat soldier. Laced around the gravel-filled parade ground is an Engineering Corps tent (very popular following Operation Desert Storm and the nuclear, biological, and chemical [NBC] warfare scare that struck Israel, as well as thirty-nine Iraqi

"Hook up. . . . Get ready. . . . JUMP!" Sayeret Tzanhanim trainees enjoy but one of the many distinc- *tions that make theirs a premier IDF reconnaissance formation.*

SCUD missiles), an Artillery Corps tent, an Armored Corps exhibition complete with a Merkava (Chariot) main battle tank, and even a Military Police tent. The Golani and Giva'ati Infantry Brigades are also well represented—as is the regular conscript paratroop brigade—by a tremendous wooden cutout of the silver metal jump wings and an imposing "winged snake" brigade emblem.

Then, of course, is Sayeret Tzanhanim's tent, adorned only by a small replica of the unit's reconnaissance wings and a jeep bedazzled by three mounted FN MAG 7.62mm light machine guns, a few jerry cans, and sophisticated-looking bits of communications gear emitting a hypnotic serenade of squelchlike noises. The recruits, looking as green as new soldiers can in poorly fitting olive-drab fatigues, are mesmerized. The principal exhibit at the Sayeret Tzanhanim tent is, of course, First Sergeant Eyal, the charismatic NCO charged with convincing the young men assembled before him that trying out for the Sayeret is a challenge worth everyone's time and effort. Leaning against a shaky rectangular folding table covered by a crusty piece of canvas, First Sergeant Eyal looks almost regal in his bright red beret and close-cropped jet black hair, loose-fitting and unironed Class A jump smock, and baggy trousers. An instructor's lanyard connects his left shoulder, bearing the paratroop brigade's winged snake unit patch, to his left breast pocket, which is itself

Winter warfare, Sayeret Tzanhanim style: reconnaissance paratroopers, looking somewhat "Nordic" in their waterproof coveralls and ski masks, march up the snow cliffs of Mt. Hermon during nighttime exercises.

adorned by regular jump wings and the smaller, though much more important, reconnaissance wings below. He is, however, no Rambo, no mighty figure of muscle meant to intimidate. He isn't a particularly tall man, only 5ft, 9in; he hasn't been pumping too much iron; and he appears more soft-spoken than threatening. Yet something in his manner makes him a man to be reckoned with. He has definite presence. His eyes are focused and piercing. His cutting-edge manner is made all the more evident by his incessant—and annoying—habit of flicking the safety switch from full safety to semiautomatic on his Glilon short-automatic rifle (SAR).

First Sergeant Eyal uses the same speech every time he addresses a group of young recruits. He stares at each young and naive face and informs the assembled that 99 percent of those sitting inside the tent will never make it to Sayeret Tzanhanim. He says:

> They don't have the right stuff. Sayeret Tzanhanim is a family—a conglomerate of men who have pushed themselves beyond the limit of their bodies and minds and have taken hold of the situation that they are the true cutting edge of the Israeli military. Forget about the other military formations in the Army, forget about the other Sayerot. Sayeret Tzanhanim is the best that there is. We are a small unit—only a few dozen Sayarim [Recon Scouts]. In fact, we don't need many men to fill our needs this conscription period. What we do require is that you be the best that you can be, and that you provide us with a 100% "Sayeret effort." We don't expect a man who can march 120km carrying an RPG and a load of rockets right out of Ba'Ku'M, but if you push yourself to try it, you *might* be exactly what we are looking for. I don't know which one of you fit[s] our needs, but if you think you're man enough to give it a try, tell the Sayeret Tzanhanim conscription officers sitting outside the paratroop section that you want to try out for Sayeret Tzanhanim, and *we'll* contact you.

In one final PR move, First Sergeant Eyal removes the cloth covering from the table and reveals a few dozen exotic weapons that are typically carried by a paratrooper in the Sayeret, including a Soviet-produced AKMS 7.62mm assault rifle, a Glilon SAR fitted with a laser aim-point device, an M-16 adorned with a night sight for a sniper, an FN MAG, an RPG, and several other grenades and other bits of goodies that, First Sergeant Eyal explains, "are top-secret, and mention of which should not leave this tent!"

First Sergeant Eyal usually fields a question or two, and they usually revolve around some sort of horror story that the conscripts have heard about Sayeret Tzanhanim training or concern the unit's operational history. "What was it like your first time across 'enemy' lines?" "How long is basic training?" "Do the commanders *abuse* you physically or mentally in basic training?" One question involved the operational workings of a laser sighting device attached to the barrel of a Glilon and whether it really helped during nighttime operations. First Sergeant Eyal smiled to himself and then said, in a soft and sarcastic tone, "If you make it to the Sayeret, don't worry, you'll spend most of your awake hours freezing your asses off in nighttime operations." First Sergeant Eyal was speaking from experience. He was one of the soldiers from Capt. Yaron Yogav's force that participated in the November 19, 1990, ambush near Ein A'ta.

First Sergeant Eyal's sincerity creates an infrangible bond between himself and the young recruits. They are savvy enough to see that one day a year or two ago, Eyal was a naive young person like themselves, and something happened to mature him in a devastating short time. Virtually every one of them rushes to the adjacent Tzanhanim building, where dozens of candidates are signing up for a chance to volunteer into the regular conscript brigade and dozens more are signing up for the Sayeret. At a table filled with personnel files are four Sayeret Tzanhanim commandos, all comrades of First Sergeant Eyal, all wearing their jump and recon wings, all proudly wearing the winged snake unit patch, and sitting beneath a sign that states the obvious: Pa'am Tzanhan—Tamid Tzanhan, or Once a Paratrooper—Always a Paratrooper.

According to several IDF studies, over 75 percent of all the conscripts who volunteer into the regular paratroop brigade actually want to serve in the Sayeret. For the new inductees to the rigors of life in the IDF—especially its elite units—who follow First Sergeant Eyal's advice and volunteer for a spot in Sayeret Tzanhanim find that his words were 100 percent accurate. The unit only needs a few select new members, and it will weed out those unfit and undesirable for service in the paratrooper Sayeret through the process of a Gibush, a three-day-long test period, where the prospective recon commandos are pushed beyond all limits of endurance to prove their worth. IDF and Sayeret Tzanhanim commanders realize that new conscripts into the IDF, having spent their first 24 or 48 hours inside the confused and chaotic confines of Ba'Ku'M, are already broken individuals. The first few nights away from home are challenge enough for most young people, but if they are going to be members of the Sayeret,

responsible for conducting dangerous and top-secret operations behind enemy lines, they will have to be able to endure an incessant array of life-threatening challenges in the years to come. "The Gibush," says Captain Y., a Sayeret officer and Gibush architect, "is a filter. Nothing else. It separates all those we can use from all those who should find employment elsewhere in the IDF." Competition for a spot on the "team" is fierce, brutal, and unforgiving. Only a few dozen are needed from a field of 100 or so hopefuls.

From the moment Sayeret Tzanhanim makes its selection and calls up all those whose physical and psychotechnical scores are high enough, the

A Sayeret Tzanhanim team leader attends to one of his own "injured" in the exercise and organizes a stretcher party to ferry the casualty to the company aid station. Israeli fallen and wounded are never left behind.

Sayeret candidates lose their identity and any semblance of individuality. The group of Sayeret hopefuls is taken to the Wingate Institute, a high-tech military sports center where physical fitness and improving a soldier's combat ability are attended to with religious zeal. When the Sayeret aspirants board their bus from Ba'Ku'M and enter the world of the paratrooper, each has a small white sign complete with a number pinned to the uniform. From that point on, "David" from Jerusalem becomes "No. 18;" "Uzi" from the northern Kibbutz at Misgav Am is "No. 30." For the duration of their Gibush, they will only be addressed by their number and will be advised against calling other Gibush hopefuls by *their* first name.

Once roll call is completed, the candidates begin their three-day-long journey into hell. A run around the base, a forced march, pushups, sit-ups, and other exercises let the candidates know that Sayeret Tzanhanim means business. It is a period of inspections, a fast-paced existence that holds no similarity to the civilian world.

The first dozen or so dropouts from the Gibush are those who came unprepared physically. The first 4km run damages them; the first forced march, at night, destroys them. Humbly, they voluntarily remove themselves from the test period and head back to Ba'Ku'M. They might still find a place with the "regular" Tzanhanim, although most come to the bitter realization that they are simply not Sayeret, or even paratrooper, material. Disappointed, angered, and feeling a bit less bombastic than when they entered the IDF, they will next try out for a spot in the Golani or Giva'ati Infantry Brigade, or even a job as a tank soldier.

During the Gibush, the Sayeret hopefuls are monitored for nearly 24 hours a day. Most participants are weeded out immediately. The Sayeret Tzanhanim officers watching the proceedings along the Mediterranean beach at Wingate, with a great degree of interest and a small degree of cruelty, can quickly distinguish between those with no potential and those who will make excellent commandos.

As the field of Sayeret candidates dwindles, the Gibush commanders have some fun. They tell the remaining brave ones to stand inside a circle.

As an officer—usually an imposing looking fellow whose granite chest is adorned with a multitude of campaign ribbons and wings—blows a whistle, each Sayeret hopeful must violently evict the other soldiers from the circle. The principle is simple. The one who remains wins; this victor is usually invited to begin the seemingly unending Sayeret Tzanhanim basic training.

The madness and jollying at the Gibush continues until the unit has all the men it can train, and then the reconnaissance commandos back at Ba'Ku'M fold their tent and head back to operational duty. Most of the new soldiers who are not accepted into the Sayeret find a varying degree of consolation. Not all their work has been in vain; they will begin training with the regular paratroopers. Service in the Sayeret may now be only a dream of what might have been, but they would still be Tzanhanim.

The specific training regimen for Sayeret Tzanhanim is highly classified, as is the case with virtually every other IDF elite unit. The candidates, of course, follow the standard infantry training of physical instruction; training with assault weapons such as the M-16, the CAR-15 and Galil 5.56mm family, the FN MAG 7.62mm light machine gun, the new Negev 5.56mm light machine gun, the M-21 7.62mm accurized sniper rifle, the RPG and LAW antitank weapons, grenades, and a wide assortment of mortars; combat assault training; survival instruction; parachutist training; and other assorted bits of commando trade craft that need to be mastered before the Sayeret Tzanhanim recon commando would be despatched into the field. Each segment in their instruction is divided by a forced march—it is a mandatory rite of passage that every paratrooper, especially one on the Sayeret, must endure. Before the soldiers receive their weapon, toward the end of their commando instruction, they undergo a forced march of varying ferocity and length. Before the soldiers receive their unit tag, they make another march. One of the most brutal of such exercises is known as the Masa'a Kumta, or Beret March. The marches can vary in length from only 30km in the beginning to 50, 60, 70, and even 120km. Sayeret Tzanhanim commanders realize that, for the most part, these troopers will be forced to reach their objectives on

With his gas mask securely fastened to his personal equipment, a Sayeret Tzanhanim trooper fires his 60mm mortar during exercises in southern Israel at the time of Operation Desert Storm and the unit's possible deployment to western Iraq.

foot, and the ability to withstand the grueling physical toll will probably save the soldiers' life behind enemy lines. They also realize that these skills must be achieved slowly—and with a touch of civility. During the Beret March, for example, the reconnaissance paratroopers are allowed to carry radio–tape players and blare their rock music, along with hauling their assault rifles, web gear, and jerry cans filled to capacity with water.

The most important term in Sayeret Tzanhanim is the word *Tzevet*, or team. Although most conventional IDF formations are divided into squads, platoons, companies, and so forth, Sayeret Tzanhanim is separated by teams: small groups of riflemen, grenadiers, and machine gunners who must operate cohesively in the field as well as back at base. The team is basically a family unit, and acceptance is everything. Like two police officers walking a beat in a dangerous portion of a city, the team members must look out for each other in the thick of a combat situation—it is a case of "you watch my back, I'll watch yours," only this time it is done with RPGs and heavy machine guns. The team means pressure. The soldiers must not just do their duty as full-time members of Sayeret Tzanhanim, but also show their loyalty to their fellow team members; anything else can result in a commando's humiliating expulsion from the unit.

Beyond the intricacies of training, the personality of the team, and other nonessentials, combat is the true essence of Sayeret Tzanhanim's existence. Once again away from the Intifadah and a step or so before the Purple Line, a formation of commandos from Sayeret Tzanhanim was conducting training exercises in the snowy steeps of Mt. Hermon. During the 1973 War, as virtually the entire Golani Brigade was carrying out its deadly battle to reclaim the peak from Syrian commandos, elements of the Tzanhanim were heli-lifted to the Syrian summit in an airborne pincer movement. The paratroopers' bond to the mountain, probably the most strategic stretch of real estate in Israel, remains infrangible, as these wintertime maneuvers certainly indicate. Several are dressed in their special white coveralls that make them look more like Norwegian special forces than Israelis; others, wearing one-piece olive waterproof coveralls, look as if they should be frolicking in the snow on a day off from school rather than checking their weapons and readying antitank rifle grenades. Many of the commandos wear woolen black ski masks—a bit of uniform that adds a small level of intimidation to their presence.

Today's mission is typical Sayeret Tzanhanim fare: they will be ferried to a point just below Mt. Hermon's peak by IAF transport choppers, climb up the unforgiving snow-capped cliffs, and then assault the "enemy" (Golani Brigade) fortifications. At the staging area, somewhere on the Golan Heights, a force of a few dozen soldiers have been gathered for several hours already. It is freezing atop the volcanic plateau, not the type of climate that desert warriors are at all fond of. A few jeeps mill about the area, and a few fighters are sharpening knives, while others perform final weapons checks. Several of the troopers go over their equipment to make sure that they haven't forgotten anything: ammunition, grenades, canteens filled to capacity, medical supplies, food, and even plastic bags for disposing of body wastes. The commandos realize the importance of this exercise, to perfect the crucial art of coordination between the paratroopers and the Air Force so that such operations, be they in 50-degree-Celsius heat or subfreezing cold, can be executed successfully during wartime.

Moments before they are to begin with the exercise, Captain Sh., the Sayeret Tzanhanim commander, addresses his troopers. Such a close-knit unit has little room for the trappings of military protocol. No salutes are given. Captain Sh. is soft-spoken and views his soldiers as comrades, rather than subordinates. There is, however, no collapse of respect. Captain Sh. is an exemplary combat leader; his past exploits and quiet and stern demeanor have made him an icon, a man the commandos would do just about anything for. He has earned their loyalty through his presence, not as a result of the three bars he wears on his epaulets. Although beloved, Captain Sh. is not a great orator, and his speech is short and concise. He reviews each team's mission and explains the importance of staying close together in the march up the mountain. "This is not a walk along the beach with your girlfriend," he mentions sarcastically. "The conditions are dangerous and should be taken seriously. You are all to stick close together, coordinate your movements, and no one is to get lost. We have too much work tonight to look for anybody with their heads up their ass." Captain Sh.'s speech is followed by a few words from Major R., the chief IAF liaison and CH-53 pilot. He simply warns the commandos against getting too close to the whirling rotor blades, especially in the snowy confines of Mt. Hermon. Major R.'s final words are "Be'Hatzlacha!"—"Good luck!"

Minutes later, the commandos disappear into the distance. They sprint to their awaiting choppers, and the aircraft lift off once all are inside their respective choppers. The flight is brief, but the change in elevation and climate is obvious. The choppers land, and the commandos quickly disappear behind a series of snow-covered rocks to organize. They must walk slowly so as not to slip in the foot-deep snow, and they must follow a definite path in order to evade the gauntlet of land mines that pepper the area. Snipers, armed with M-21s, lead the formation to eliminate any sentries—they are ordered to "remove a head" in the first shot. Snipers, after all, rarely get a second chance. The commandos must also move slowly so as not to perspire too greatly and risk later problems. They are able to negotiate the precarious terrain effectively; they have, in the past, marched hundreds of kilometers in a single burst of leg power, so what is a little snow? As they approach their target, their stealthy movement has paid off. They have yet to be detected. Captain Sh. assumes the point position from a team of snipers and grenadiers and, with a CAR-15 in one hand and the other hand raised, says, "Follow me." The enemy fortification is assaulted and neutralized in less than 5 minutes.

The remainder of the exercise is to see how long it takes for the paratroop commandos to withdraw from the battle zone. To make matters more realistic, several commandos are identified as "wounded" and carried back to the helicopter rendezvous by stretcher-bearers. Although carrying a wounded comrade and negotiating the snow is a difficult task, especially following the initial climb, it is a skill that had better be mastered. Wounded soldiers are never left on the battlefield.

The commandos reach their loading zone with little difficulty and fly back to the staging area—mission accomplished. They will return back to base, remove their wet uniforms, and warm up with some Turkish coffee. Sleep time will be brief, however. Tomorrow they are scheduled to undergo some urban combat training. Perhaps, in view of the exercise's positive outcome, Captain Sh. will let his troopers sleep a little longer. That is not likely, however. After all, this is Sayeret Tzanhanim.

The exercise was a brilliant success, but such maneuvers are meant to prepare Sayeret Tzanhanim for a full-scale conventional war that might be fought soon between the IDF and the Syrian Army. The IDF is incessantly fighting other wars, however, along the desolate Lebanese frontier or in the alleyways of the Intifadah. As the Middle East edges closer to the brink, and deadlier weapons are now in the hands of more and more enemies of the Jewish State, it appears as if Sayeret Tzanhanim's work has only just begun.

After the paratroopers!

Chapter 3

The Naval Commandos: Batmen

One summer's night at Belgia, a popular Tel Aviv eating spot and watering hole, a table in a darkencd corner is occupied by six men, all wearing khaki Class A uniforms and stark navy blue berets adorned with a gold metal beret badge bearing the words *Heyl Ha'Yam*, the Hebrew term for IDF Navy. Each soldier wears three gold cloth stripes, indicating that they are sergeants, all in active duty for nearly two years. In a boisterous, beer-induced state, they sing their folk songs with zealous fervor

After hitting the beach from its Zodiac craft, a force of naval commandos prepares to set out "deep behind enemy lines" during infiltration exercises.

and stomp their feet in rhythm, although they have to be careful with their movements, as each soldier's AK-47 7.62mm assault rifle is positioned solemnly under the table.

For the outside observer, these men appear to be nothing more than drunken sailors enjoying a brief liberty. But at closer examination, they are much more. They are quite special. Above his left breast pocket, each soldier wears a silver metal

During a religious celebration at their home base, a few of the IDF Navy's first underwater warriors carry the Torah to the rabbi. The first naval commandos may have been trailblazers, mavericks, and rogue warriors, but they realized the importance of tradition—after all, as the saying goes, "There are no atheists in foxholes."

bat wing, the symbol of the mysterious unit known, according to reports, as Shayetet 13, or Flotilla 13, the IDF Navy's naval commando unit. The parachutist wings above the right breast pocket indicates that these men are much more than underwater warriors. They are capable of engaging the enemy on any terms, in any conditions, and in the most unexpected places. No one else in the pub watching these naval commandos bending their elbows knows why they are singing; is it because they are just out having a good time, or is it because they have successfully returned from a covert operation on a heavily fortified enemy beach? Flotilla 13 is, indeed, a mystery.

Flotilla 13—or Ha'Kommando Ha'Yami, as it is more commonly referred to in Israel—is an enigma, even though it is an important, specialized, and spectacular Israeli special force. For years, little mention has been made of it in either the Israeli media or foreign news reports. Because of the covert nature of its work and the confidentiality of its training and methods of operation, Flotilla 13 has had to remain protected by a veil of self-imposed inviolable secrecy. Only in April 1988, when foreign reports highlighted Flotilla 13's role in the Israeli assassination of Abu Jihad, deputy commander of the PLO, in Tunis, did the unit receive any degree of recognition and mention. Ever since, however, small slivers of the naval commandos' veil of secrecy have begun to peel away—ever so slowly.

Even though the activities, operations, and, for the most part, personality of this unit have been hidden from public scrutiny, Flotilla 13 is one of the oldest military units in the IDF. Its history goes back to the Pal'mach, World War II, and a group of Israeli underwater trailblazers.

In November 1940, the British Special Operations Executive (SOE) sanctioned the formation of a commando unit that centered around the Haganah's best fighters—all volunteers—to conduct seaborne intelligence-gathering and sabotage operations behind Axis lines in the Mediterranean. The Jewish fighters were the nucleus of the Pal'mach, the fifth-column guerrilla force pioneered as a joint British-Jewish contingency plan for the expected Nazi invasion of Palestine. Covertly, this unit was trained by the SOE in a Tel

Aviv park in amphibious warfare, underwater skills, and commando techniques. On the night of May 18, 1941, twenty-three frogmen, commanded by Maj. Anthony Palmer, boarded the Her, or His, Majesty's Ship (H.M.S.) *Sea Lion* and set out from Haifa for international waters; their objective was the destruction of the Vichy French oil refineries in Tripoli, Lebanon. The *Sea Lion* never reached Tripoli, and the fate of the twenty-three men remains a mystery to this day. Although their doomed mission was a miniscule chapter in the history of the Second World War, the "23" were Israel's first naval commandos.

In 1943, after the Pal'mach's German and Syrian Platoons helped the war effort in Syria, Lebanon, and North Africa, an indigenous naval element, called the Pal'yam, or Sea Companies, was formed; its mysterious Ha'Huliyah Ha'Yamit, or Sea Section, served as the first Israeli naval commando unit. The commanders of the Pal'mach wished to base their seaborne commando force along the lines of the British Special Boat Service (SBS) and its legendary Cockleshell Heros, but the Jews possessed neither a great naval heritage nor a lavish supply of arms. In fact, the first Pal'mach soldiers "forced" to volunteer into the Sea Section

The gold metal beret badge worn by every naval commando: Heyl Ha'Yam. Sigalit Katz

had to fulfill only two requirements: minimal sea experience and ownership of their own small fishing vessel.

Through Spartan beginnings, the Pal'yam's Sea Section grew into a recognizable and somewhat capable force. On the shores of the Mediterranean, the Pal'yam established an underground training facility to teach its commandos to counter the British naval efforts against refugee ships bringing Holocaust survivors to Palestine. Poorly armed and equipped—the divers wore inadequate wet suits and carried explosives that were extremely volatile—the Sea Section crippled a Royal Navy patrol craft, the H.M.S. *Empire Rival*, with limpet mines on August 21, 1946, and the H.M.S. *Ocean Vigour* off the Cypriot coast on March 3, 1947.

Following the withdrawal of British forces from Palestine and the subsequent war for Israel's independence, the underwater commandos of the Pal'mach were significant combatants against both the irregular Palestinian forces and the conventional Arab navies. Initially, the Pal'mach's special naval units participated in military operations unique to a newly created state desperately

Wearing their black neoprene wet suits, a force of naval commandos, Uzi submachine guns in hand, practice assaulting a heavily fortified target from the sea during the War of Attrition prior to the assault on Green Island.

in search of weapons. Three operations against a shipment of Czech arms to Syria onboard an Italian vessel, the S.S. *Lino*—Operation Spoils 1, 2, and 3, April 2–10, 1948—were carried out by twenty-five naval commandos from the Pal'mach's 4th Battalion, the body commanding the Pal'yam and all Pal'mach special operations, which roamed the Mediterranean for the *Lino* on a floating base, the Haganah ship *South Africa*. On the night of April 9–10, the Pal'mach divers located the *Lino* docked in Bari, Italy, and sank the overloaded vessel with crude, though effective, Haganah-produced limpet mines. The Italians salvaged the *Lino*, and the arms were transferred to another ship, the S.S. *Argero*, which was eventually seized in the middle of the Mediterranean by the infant IDF Navy, and its cargo of 8,000 rifles and 8 million rounds of ammunition was unloaded at Haifa harbor on August 29, 1948.

At the height of the 1948 War, the IDF Navy possessed two naval commando units: the Frogman Unit, commanded by Yosef Dror, who directed the *Lino* operation, and the Sabotage Craft Unit, commanded by Yochai Ben-Nun, which primarily deployed from an Italian MTM-type (Pig) explosive craft carrying 250kg of high explosives in its hull. To complement the training on the MTM craft, which was carried out on the Sea of Galilee, the IDF Navy employed a firebrand former Italian naval commando officer, Fiorenco Caprioti, who secretly trained the force in the choppy Mediterranean waters. Compared with the remainder of the IDF, which consisted of aging men and newly conscripted immigrants, or most of the fighters in the Pal'mach, who were the idealistic elite of the new state, the soldiers of the IDF Navy's Frogman and Sabotage Craft Units were mavericks and adventurers. In special operations, however, they remained untested until October 21, 1948, when they participated in a spectacular operation of the 1948 War.

Just before the start of the IDF's Operation Yoav—a five-brigade offensive, October 15–21, 1948, that eventually ousted the Royal Egyptian Army from the Negev Desert—the IDF General Staff was concerned about Egyptian naval craft that might make an appearance and impede the IDF advance. They duly ordered the sabotage unit to attack Egyptian shipping; but first it had to find the Egyptians! For days, IDF Navy warships patrolled the waters off the Gaza Strip in search of the Egyptian Navy, and on October 21, they found more than they expected: the Royal Egyptian Navy Ship (R.E.N.S.) *Emir Farouk*, a destroyer, was spotted along the Mediterranean coast with an escorting mine sweeper.

At 2100 hours, three MTM craft and a collection vessel were discharged from the Israel Navy Ship (I.N.S.) *Maoz* into the choppy pitch black Mediterranean. One MTM was ordered to attack the *Farouk;* the other MTM headed toward the mine sweeper; and the third MTM, directed by unit commander Ben-Nun, would wait in the water to determine which target required additional attention. The commandos wore special reflectors affixed to their khaki caps and would be picked up in midwater by a collection vessel equipped with special visual devices.

The first MTM headed straight for the *Farouk* and, although the driver had initial trouble releasing himself with the flotation device from the speeding craft, it scored a direct hit. Contrary to the plans, however, the other craft also directed itself toward the *Farouk* and scored a hit, too. Left alone in this enveloping chaos and in the uncontrollable seas was unit commander Ben-Nun, who was forced to guide his ship against the mine sweeper, which, now alerted to the Israeli attackers, began pouring heavy machine gun fire in Ben-Nun's direction. Courageously, Ben-Nun continued his efforts against the mine sweeper, and, although he, too, encountered difficulties in releasing himself from the MTM, he scored a direct hit—sinking the ship in a thunderous blast. For his courage in the command and execution of the operation, Ben-Nun was awarded the I'tur Ha'Gvura medal for bravery—the IDF's highest reward for valor and the first of many commendations naval commandos would receive in the years to come.

Following the 1948 War, Ha'Kommando Ha'Yami sank into a mysterious aura of deep secrecy and obscurity. It received little press coverage and was never mentioned in public. In fact, severe debates took place within the Israeli defense community as to how to use "Flotilla 13."

Some within the IDF wanted to form a special commando corps, much like a special forces brigade, under the command of former Pal'mach officers. Others, including Dror and Ben-Nun, wanted Flotilla 13 to consist of over 500 fighters and to be separate not only from the Navy, but from the IDF as well. They envisioned the naval commandos as a highly covert special operations and intelligence force, under the command of the Defense Ministry and available for special tasks in concert with A'man (IDF Military Intelligence) and Mossad (Israel's foreign-espionage service) activities abroad.

Ha'Kommando Ha'Yami remained in the IDF, however, and returned to its intensive training routine. Its training was divided into two distinctive portions: naval assault and underwater opera-

Maj. Gen. Ze'ev Almog, IDF Navy commander from 1981 to 1984 and an influential naval commando officer.

51

tions, and paratroop infantry maneuvers. In fact, many of the IDF paratroopers who jumped at the Mitla Pass on October 31, 1956, were naval commandos undergoing a squad leaders course with the 890th Paratroop Batallion commanded by Maj. Rafael ("Raful") Eitan. During the 1956 War, units from Flotilla 13 conducted reconnaissance and sabotage missions along Sinai's Mediterranean and Red Sea coasts, and in 1958, it conducted a daring deep-penetration raid against the port of Beirut.

The naval commandos' lack of publicity was not an indication of their lack of activity. Theirs was a close-knit force of professionals in for the duration who perfected their unit's abilities for hit-and-run attacks through torturing trial and error. Several innovative tactics were also attempted, including deployment in kayaks from S-55 helicopters. They also trained abroad, including stints with the British SBS and Royal Marines as well as with the French and Italian underwater military units. As a volunteer force, Flotilla 13 accepted only the strongest and most intelligent conscripts. All of its members needed the basic faculties of command as well as the courage and determination to survive basic training and beyond. Most of the volunteers, like those who flocked to

Hitting the shore hard, a force of naval commandos advances quickly and decisively up an "enemy" beach during maneuvers in central Israel.

join other IDF reconnaissance units, came from the Kibbutzim.

During the 1967 Six Day War, Flotilla 13 finally entered the public spotlight. On June 5, at 1900 hours, six frogmen exited an IDF Navy submarine, the I.N.S. *Tanin*, or *Crocodile*, several kilometers north of the Egyptian port of Alexandria, on the southern Mediterranean, and set out for an audacious mission in the opening hours of the conflict: the destruction of Egyptian naval vessels anchored in the port, with limpet mines. The six-person team, which swam for Alexandria in three groups of two, had trained long and hard for the operation, and the unit commander, Lt. Col. Aharon ("Eskimo") Ben-Yosef, felt they were more than ready to execute such a dangerous mission. From the onset, however, the commandos encountered severe difficulties. The Egyptians expected an Israeli attack, and sailors from Coast Guard vessels lobbed menacing depth charges and hand grenades into the water. This forced the team toward the coastline and a submerged cave where they found temporary shelter. They had yet to execute their task and were already 3 hours beyond their rendezvous with the *Tanin* when they were encountered by a mob of spear-wielding Egyptian fishermen! The six attempted to pass themselves off as British commercial divers but were soon led away into custody, where they were interrogated and brutally tortured; they kept their military composure and discipline, only disclosing the required name, rank, and serial number. They were eventually exchanged in a prisoner swap.

The same day, a force of naval commandos led by Maj. Ze'ev Almog—a future commander of Flotilla 13 as well as the IDF Navy—exited the IDF Navy's flagship, the I.N.S. *Eilat*, for a sabotage mission against Port Said, the Suez Canal's opening to the Mediterranean. The force, using Zodiac craft, reached the target undetected but failed to find any ships in port. Similar aborted forays were conducted against the Syrian ports of Latakia and Tartus. The only known time that the naval commandos participated in combat during the 1967 War, in fact, was when an ad hoc force of naval commandos attached themselves to the 80th Paratroop (Reserve) Brigade during the attack on the Golan Heights on June 9, 1967.

During the brutal 1967–70 1,000 Days War of Attrition, Flotilla 13 truly came into its own as a special operations combat force—especially under the command of Lieutenant Colonel Almog, a seventeen-year veteran of the force who urged the IDF General Staff for a greater combat role for his commandos. The unit's first publicized offensive mission was Operation Mania 5, an attack on the Egyptian Red Sea coastal radar facility at Ras al-Adabia. The objective was a formidable target; according to A'man reports, the position was heavily defended by between thirty and fifty Egyptian soldiers and a complement of 130mm artillery pieces and stationary antiaircraft guns.

The naval commandos trained hard for the operation, often perfecting their assault techniques for over 20 hours a day. Under a war-darkened sky on the night of June 21, 1969, seven loaded-down Zodiac craft set out from their Sinai base at Ras Masala. The force consisted of twenty commandos divided into five teams of four, including a four-person fire team equipped with FN MAG 7.62mm light machine guns and 52mm mortars. The attack force was equipped with special electronic sensors to detect Egyptian radar. After approaching to within earshot of the shallow waters just off the coast, they cut their engines and crawled—for 30 minutes—to shore. The lead force cut all telephone lines and mined routes of a possible Egyptian counterattack, while the assault contingent struck from a northern approach. Two Egyptian sentries enjoying a smoke were immediately eliminated with bursts of 7.62mm fire from the commandos' AK-47s, and soon, dozens of Egyptians raced into the desert in panic. Twelve minutes later, the base was destroyed; thirty-two Egyptians were killed, and dozens wounded. The success of Operation Mania 5 was a rousing boost of morale for the naval commandos, which, following its less-than-glowing performance in the 1967 War, needed to prove its worth. The success of Operation Mania 5 also ensured future work for the IDF Navy's underwater warriors.

In response to increased Egyptian commando activity against IDF positions along the Suez Canal, and a particularly brutal attack against a Bar Lev line position in which several soldiers were killed and several officers kidnapped, the IDF General Staff decided to retaliate harshly in a manner that would expose Egyptian vulnerability and undermine Egyptian morale and resolve. The target chosen was the imposing al-Ahdar, or Green Island, a human-built 100-meter-long island in the middle of the southern approach to the Suez Canal, protected by four 85mm and two 137mm antiaircraft guns. The defenders included eighty soldiers, including elite al-Saiga (Thunderbolt) commandos.

Attacking a target so isolated and surrounded by water was extremely difficult. It was too risky to make an amphibious assault, since the position's heavy guns would cut down any flotilla of Zodiac craft racing for its walls. As a result, Ze'ev Almog and Raful Eitan, chief paratroop and infantry officer, decided that the assault, code named Operation Mania 6, would be carried out in two distinctive and unusual stages. First, twenty naval commandos would *swim* to their objective, stealthily securing a landing zone for the second

Following one of the most difficult training courses in existence, a new group of fighters joins Israel's family of naval commandos at the unit's home base somewhere in Israel.

wave, a force of twenty reconnaissance paratroopers from Sayeret Mat'kal that would attack the position and wipe out the defenders. For days, the combined force of naval commandos and recon paratroopers trained incessantly on "mock targets," such as police forts and even a crusader castle, in central Israel. The naval commandos practiced swimming underwater for extended periods of time with over 30kg of weaponry and ammunition; they also trained in the accurate firing of their Uzis and AK-47s upon emerging from the water. Two days prior to the attack, the commandos were flown to Sinai for a final review before the IDF top brass. The offensive was scheduled for the night of July 19–20, 1969.

At 1945 hours, the commandos put their boats in the water. Each fighter wore only the top portion of a wet suit—which protected the swimmer against the cold water as well as provided buoyancy—over a Dacron fatigue blouse and trousers; the regular uniform would dry quickly once outside the water and would also be more comfortable for the anticipated close-quarter, hand-to-hand combat. The difficulties in reaching the target underwater, however, were enormous; the responsibility lay with Lieutenant I., the commander of the "Flotilla 13" training course and the officer responsible for navigation. He had difficulties leading his four squads—each consisting of two officers and three NCOs—through the

After the jump wings have taken second place above their right breast pocket and the coveted naval commando bat wings have been pounded into their chest, a new force of underwater warriors join some senior members of the Ha'Kommando Ha'Yami club and salute the Israeli flag.

placid waters, since all the fighters carried additional loads of explosives and ammunition, and the commandos encountered problems in staying afloat at a safe depth, especially since they were breathing pure oxygen.

At 0138 hours, after an arduous swim, the force reached the island's round tower and was ready for action. Each fighter cocked a weapon underwater; specially modified bangalore torpedoes were readied, and the divers' breathing apparatus systems and masks were removed; and wire cutters were prepared to cut through the main fence's breach. In fact, everything was going according to plan when a sentry appeared and Lieutenant I. instinctively opened fire. Immediately, the entire island erupted into a massive and chaotic firefight; grenade fragments and tracers illuminated the dark skies. Since the diving depths their overloaded pouches had brought them to had rendered many of the RPGs and grenades inoperable, the underwater attackers had to advance, climb over positions, and contend with the overwhelming Egyptian firepower until the Sayeret force arrived. Systematically, the commandos neutralized the Egyptian positions with courage and determination. After a command post was established, a green flare was fired and Lieutenant Colonel Almog, who was with the reconnaissance paratroopers in midwater, ordered in the Mat'kal commandos; they encountered stiff and deadly resistance. Thirty minutes and much heavy fighting later, the attack force planted over 80kg of explosives throughout the position and made a hasty, even chaotic, retreat with the Zodiac craft. As IDF artillery shells began to pound the island, it exploded in a thunderous blast.

Although the operation, in the words of Eitan, "had broken the backs of the Egyptian[s] in the War of Attrition," it was controversial in its dear price. Three naval commandos died at Green Island, as did three Mat'kal recon fighters; dozens more were seriously wounded. The loss of six of the IDF's best fighters in attacking what many consider a secondary target at best made the operation controversial; news of the attack was suppressed by military censors for many years, although its significance in how the IDF mounts its special operations, as well as how it selects its targets, has lasted until today.

Although the war of attrition against the conventional Arab armies of Egypt, Syria and Jordan "ended" in a series of cease-fire accords, Israel's war of attrition against Palestinian terrorism intensified and expanded. Two spectacular IDF special operations against terrorism involved Flotilla 13. The first was the February 20, 1973, Operation Hood 54–55, a joint paratroop–naval commando raid on a series of Palestinian terrorist bases, 180km from the Israeli frontier, around the city of Tripoli, Lebanon—the targets centered around the al-Badawi and Nahar al-Bard refugee camps. The raid followed the 1972 Munich Olympic Massacre, when, according to foreign sources, Mossad hit teams roamed Europe for retribution against Black September activities and IDF retaliatory attacks on Palestinian terrorist targets in Lebanon and Syria were commonplace. The raid on Tripoli was, in fact, three distinctive operations, with the naval commandos assigned the destruction of PLO Force 17, Yasir Arafat's Praetorian guard; the PLO's terrorist training center for "international pupils," which Flotilla 13 attacked along with a force of reconnaissance paratroopers; and the principal headquarters of the PFLP. A rumored side objective was the assassination of Dr. George Habash, a PFLP warlord, who was reported to be in the camp that evening. The combined task force was ferried to its objective by IDF Navy missile boats and then to shore by Zodiac craft. It reached its inland targets after a precarious forced march through hostile territory cut off from any heavy fire support. When the battles erupted, they were like nothing the unit had ever experienced before: fierce, unforgiving, close-quarter—pointblank!—firefights. Several naval commandos were severely wounded, including Maj. Eilan Egozzi, who lost an eye and an arm and would be awarded his second I'tur Ha'Oz bravery decoration in four years (he was also decorated in the battle for Green Island).

The next major special operation in which the naval commandos played a prominent role was the infamous Operation Spring of Youth—the attack on Beirut on April 9–10, 1973. While commandos from Sayeret Mat'kal assassinated three of the top officers of Black September and reconnaissance paratroopers attacked the headquarters of the DFLP, the naval commandos were to carry out two objectives: the first, code named Vardah, was the destruction of the el-Fatah headquarters responsible for operations inside Israel and an explosives factory; the second was the destruction of Tzilah, an ammunition dump located north of the Beirut harbor.

When the armies of Syria and Egypt launched their brilliantly coordinated surprise attack on the State of Israel to initiate the 1973 Yom Kippur War on October 6, 1973, oddly enough, the small IDF Navy was the only alert force. Although Israeli naval commando raids against the Syrian ports of Latakia and Tartus have been widely rumored, Flotilla 13's raid against Egyptian naval installations packed the greatest punch in the overall

fighting. The first attack was against the Egyptian Navy base of Port Said, on October 16–17, in which a Komar missile boat and several torpedo craft were mined; two Israeli divers never returned. The second operation was against the naval base of A'rdaka, on the southern mouth of the Suez Canal.

Flotilla 13 efforts against A'rdaka began on October 9 when the presence of an Egyptian torpedo boat led to the abortion of a raiding mission. Two days later, Flotilla 13 returned to A'rdaka and mined several vessels. Urged on by their previous success, the naval commandos returned to A'rdaka on the night of October 19–20 and, once again, severely damaged the already beleaguered base.

The final raid came on the night of October 21–22, when a large force of commandos, armed with ten American-made LAW 66mm antitank

A stoic Israeli naval commando as he prepares to launch a 40mm grenade from his unique AK-47/M203 combination after hitting the beach during maneu- *vers. Note the mask covering his face, specialized web gear, and communications equipment.*

rockets, made a final showing at A'rdaka. The acquisition of the LAWs presented new tactical flexibility to the naval commandos but came with restrictions as well—the commandos were ordered *not* to aim the missiles at the Styx Surface-to-Surface Missile (SSM) launchers on the Komar and Osa missile boats, since detonating a warhead with 500kg of high explosives would create an inferno that would certainly have enveloped the attack force. During the raid, the attack force reached to within 100m of the sprawling Egyptian base, when it was discovered and a ferocious firefight ensued. Unfortunately, the first eight LAW rockets missed by large margins, jeopardizing the mission for the entire force; the final two rockets scored direct hits, destroying a Komar in a ball of fire. This A'rdaka raid was of grand historical significance. First, it was learned that the destroyed Komar was the same ship that sank the IDF Navy flagship, the I.N.S. *Eilat*, in October 1967; second, the commandos' cover force was directed by Maj. Gen. (Reserves) Yochai Ben-Nun, the officer who, twenty-five years earlier to the day, as commander of the Sabotage Craft Unit, sank the *Emir Farouk*.

Following the 1973 War, the naval commandos returned to anonymity and its veil of secrecy. Prior to, and during, the Operation Peace for Galilee invasion of Lebanon on June 6–7, 1982, the naval commandos participated in numerous intelligence-gathering forays as well as hit-and-run attacks against Palestinian targets. On the night of June 6, 1982, they landed on the coast of Sidon and prepared a secure beachhead for the largest amphibious landing in IDF Navy history. According to many reports, they came to the Lebanese coast on countless reconnaissance forays and covert strikes; they are believed to have landed on the Awali beachhead before the Israeli landing and "removed" all Palestinian defenders from the area.

On April 16, 1988, foreign sources reported, "Flotilla 13" secured a beachhead for attacking IDF commando forces, although this time the beach was over 2,500km away from Israel in Tunis, Tunisia, and the force the unit was covering was the Sayeret Mat'kal squad that assassinated Deputy Chief Abu Jihad of the PLO. Ferried to the Tunisian coast on two IDF Navy missile boats, a group of naval commandos reached a deserted beach near Ras Carthage, swimming underwater, and quickly rendezvoused with a team of Mossad agents waiting near the surf with three rented vehicles. While the Sayeret Mat'kal commandos and Mossad intelligence agents together proceeded with their mission, the Flotilla 13 task force waited behind, securing the beachhead against any unwanted intrusion from Tunisian military units and Palestinian security forces. Foreign reports said this was familiar territory to the naval commandos. As part of their mandate as underwater intelligence gatherers, they had reconnoitered the Tunisian coastline on countless missions. The same reports said similar deep-penetration forays were mounted against other "Arab" coastlines, too.

On December 8–9, 1988, the naval commandos are reported to have secured a beachhead for the reconnaissance force from the elite Golani Brigade in a raid against the headquarters of Ahmed Jibril, commander of the PFLP-GC, which was situated in a series of Vietnamese-designed tunnels and caves at Na'ameh, near Damur.

The unique importance of the naval commandos, and the IDF Navy, is, perhaps, best expressed in the recruitment process: although the IAF has first crack at any new recruit in Ba'Ku'M, next on the list is the Navy—before the paratroopers and any other reconnaissance force. As in most other IDF elite units, conscripts make their way to the flotilla through Ba'Ku'M and only following successful completion of a Gibush. As the commandos of Flotilla 13 are proud owners of a somewhat offbeat reputation—many Israeli soldiers look upon them as certifiably crazy—the naval commando Gibush is considered an exercise of pure torture, a procedure designed to make terrified soldiers quiver and squirm in fright. According to rumor, Flotilla 13 hopefulls are submerged in a frigid tank, with a snorkel and a mask with the glass painted black, and subjected to the bites of crabs and other beasts until they can take no more. The candidates are, of course, subjected to physical and psychological examinations—especially psychological. Conscripts might be able to run through the surf of northern Israel with a 40kg sack of sand strapped to their back, but what possesses these same young persons to want to volunteer into a unit where the training, according to published reports, lasts over sixteen months and where their daily existence will consist of performing operations that no one is ever supposed to hear about, they will encounter obstacles such as limpet mines and hand grenades tossed into shallow port waters, and the risk of death on a foreign beach far from home looms ever present?

Crazy reputation aside, the naval commandos are not fanatics when it comes to selecting their people from the Gibush. After all, many months will pass before one can be ordained a full-fledged member of the unit. What the Gibush will not weed out, training and actual service in the naval commandos definitely will. According to Colonel Sh., the commander of the naval commandos in 1992, "The flotilla is searching for above-average men with the ability to *acquire* underwater and combat skills. The candidate need not be of superior physical ability, he doesn't need to be an Olympic swimmer, nor does he need to be a certified scuba diver. In fact, in the beginning, he only needs to know how to float. Motivation, desire, and other intangibles come later." The Gibush removes

Draped in their black neoprene wet suits, naval commandos deploy underwater during combat rescue exercises.

half of the volunteers from the naval commando's call; basic training will eliminate an even greater number of soldiers.

Since training is expensive and the IDF, as frugal a military force as can be found in the world, cannot afford to provide advanced and top-secret underwater training to anyone, naval commando candidates must first prove their worth as infantry fighters and paratroopers before going underwater. Indeed, the first leg of their instruction is basic paratrooper training: seven months of infantry and assault training, the squad leaders course, and parachuting. Only after they are corporals and wear parachutist wings across the chest are they introduced to the Mediterranean Sea and allowed their first "dip" into the water. It is here that paratroop-trained recruits are transformed into what Colonel Sh. calls "land and sea animals." At any point during their even lengthier instruction, naval commando candidates can be tossed from the course. Only the best become members of the flotilla, and the pressure to succeed—in the classroom, underwater, and in combat exercises—is enormous. Those who cannot persevere are either returned to the paratroopers or given another assignment in the Heyl Ha'Yam.

As one former member of Flotilla 13 said, "The unit is like a combination between a close-knit family and the Mafia: once you're in, you're in it for life." Indeed, many naval officers whose service began in the naval commandos might go through the motions of service in patrol boats and missile craft, but their heart belongs to their bat wings, their scuba gear, and the adrenaline that races

Having been briefed and issued its operational assignments, a naval commando team heads out for the refreshing depths of the Mediterranean during summer maneuvers.

through their body while assaulting an enemy beach from Zodiac craft.

Many naval commandos have extremely personal reasons for their lifelong dedication to the unit. Lieutenant Colonel D., the unit's deputy commander, wanted to be a "fighter" from the time he was a child. His father was a concentration camp survivor, and serving in a combat unit was D.'s only possible course of action to ensure that Never Again was not just a slogan; it was what motivated him when he was selected to volunteer for service in the flotilla in Ba'Ku'M, and it was what helped him persevere through the trials and tribulations of naval commando training and operations. Yet, it was during the 1973 War, when D. was but a green new member to a flotilla team, that the importance of serving in the naval commandos became clear. "It was the first time that I, as a soldier, ever felt threatened," he explained, "and the first time that as an Israeli, I felt the vulnerability of this nation; it was a sobering period."

An officer on board the I.N.S. Tanin, *one of the IDF Navy's three submarines, prepares to reach the depths in the Mediterranean. Foreign sources reported that the IDF Navy's minifleet of submarines is also used as a platform for the naval commandos' covert deployment.*

It takes a special person to allow such motivators to determine the course of life and to select service in a special and difficult unit like the flotilla. It, indeed, takes a special person to stay in such a unit for so long. Lieutenant Colonel D. achieved his relatively high rank in a remarkably short time. The two falafel leaves were pinned to his epaulet by his twenty-eighth birthday.

Since the naval commandos' next battlefield remains a mystery, the team must prepare for every contingency—any combat possibility. After all, the flotilla is, many times, the IDF's eyes and ears on the ground. It is the first unit called in when a foreign power threatens the national security of the Jewish State. To be ready once the flames of violence erupt in the area, the members of the naval commandos must train incessantly. Combat training and amphibious assaults are tasks the "batmen" attend to with religious conviction. Their fluid skills in storming a beach and proficiency with an automatic rifle will decide between the successful—and safe—execution of a mission and *failure*, a Flotilla 13 term for becoming a combat fatality.

The true mandate of the IDF Navy's naval commandos is to attack enemy coastal targets, enemy shipping, and port facilities. It is extremely dangerous work. According to Colonel Sh., the operations of the unit are not like those in an American action movie: "No one has the right to gamble with their lives." They are coordinated efforts, and each commando must be well versed in all aspects of combat, from certain technological intricacies, including demolitions and communications, to cold-killing with a dagger and sharpshooting. The choreography for this "death-from-below-the-depths" art is perfected in what is known in Hebrew as Imunim, or maneuvers.

To reach its targets, the naval commandos deploy a wide variety of means and methods—most of which are highly classified. In past operations, such as the raids on Tripoli and Beirut in 1973, naval commandos were ferried from the base in Israel to the Lebanese shore by patrol boats or missile boats. Of course, they reached the enemy beach by means of the coveted and ubiquitous Zodiac rubber dinghy. The black rubber craft, a standard in virtually every naval military formation in the world, has served the naval commandos well since the early 1950s.

It is just after midnight, on a desert beachhead somewhere in northern Israel. The full moon provides some light, but to the three lone figures emerging from the murky Mediterranean surf, the lunar floodlighting is way too much illumination. The three men, wearing neoprene wet suits and carrying scuba gear and oxygen tanks, caress the AK-47 assault rifles that they have quickly removed from plastic wrappings, race across the beach to a line of foliage located 45 meters away, and take cover. They have made absolutely no noise, and all communications between them is coordinated through hand signals and instinct. Once they have assumed camouflaged cover, they remove infrared night goggles from their carrying cases and quickly fasten laser targeting devices underneath the barrels of their AKs. They scan the area in a 180-degree radius, gazing across the quiet shoreline through the green world of infrared imagery. All is clear. They flash a beacon back to sea, and moments later, three Zodiac craft hit the surf. Before the rubber dinghies touch the sand, the commandos jump off and, in a coordinated effort, pull them toward shore with great finesse and ease. The new arrivals to this "enemy beach" are truly equipped for combat. They wear load-bearing equipment crammed with ammunition and grenades and satchels filled with plastic explosives. Their objective this night is a series of "mock" communications platforms; they are to be sabotaged, and destroyed by explosive charges.

One squad remains at the shoreline and assumes a defensive perimeter. These commandos grandish FN MAGs and RPGs and have covered all approaches to the beach; they also cover the movements of their comrades advancing another 100m inland. Everything goes well with the task. The two squads charged with destroying the facility place their explosives underneath the platform and return to the beach in under 5 minutes. Yet, as they begin sliding their Zodiacs back to the chilly depths, an alarm is sounded. They have been discovered. Several flares are launched into the heavens, and the cracking chirp of automatic fire emanates inland.

The commandos gear their engines at full throttle, but it is apparent that they need some additional firepower. Waiting a few dozen meters out at sea is a Snunit, or Swallow, a small motorized speedboat, painted olive green and capable of tremendous speeds. If the Zodiac craft is the naval commandos' jeep, then this is their Ferrari. The Snunit is also equipped with mounted FN MAGs as well as other, more explosive weapons. As the fleet of Zodiac craft races from the sea, the Snunit heads in toward the shore with its weapons ablaze. It is primarily used as a floating firebase for

High-speed action and coordination at its best: an IAF Bell-212 removes a wounded officer from a naval commando Snunit fast-attack craft.

assault teams, and it performs its mission brilliantly. Once the blanket of covering fire has "neutralized" opposing fire, the Snunit heads back out to sea. Seconds later, a tremendous explosion rocks the water. The communications platform has erupted into a fireball of destruction. Mission accomplished.

Naval commandos can be sure of two things: they will be criticized for their failures in a training mission, and they will also be criticized for their success. Nothing with Flotilla 13 is ever taken for granted. The postmission briefing can last hours and be particularly cruel. Commanders aren't keen on cementing friendships, after all; they just want to make sure that everyone returns from the mission alive.

Back at their home base, a little after 0300 hours, Colonel Sh. is writing a report about this training exercise. Both technique and execution were successful, although perfection was not achieved. As he sits in his Spartan office adorned with trophies and plaques donated by visiting naval commandos from other countries, he can hear the muted sounds of commandos jogging through the night. Realizing they are trainees undergoing a brief run before diving at night, the experienced colonel suddenly understands that this is all madness. Forcing soldiers into the

The Israel Military Industries' Negev 5.56mm light machine gun—a new tool in the naval commandos' offensive arsenal. Israel Military Industries

freezing water at night in order to acclimate them with the bone-chilling temperatures is craziness—but a dire necessity when the soldiers will find themselves not in a training environment, but rather in the thick of combat. Such madness is a tremendous burden to place on the shoulders of eighteen-year-old trainees, but, after all, he recalls, these are very special eighteen year olds.

Although the naval commandos are one of the smaller elements in today's high-tech, fast-attack-craft IDF Navy, two of the past four IDF Navy commanders have been former Flotilla 13 commanders. The first, Maj. Gen. Ze'ev Almog, assumed command of the Heyl Ha'Yam in 1981, at a time when Israel was gearing up for a full-scale showdown with the Palestinian ministate in Lebanon. A veteran naval commando with an exemplary combat record, Almog had directed several spectacular operations against Egyptian and Syrian targets; most of his operations, however, remain classified. Almog was the IDF Navy commander in June 1982, when Israel invaded Lebanon, and was instrumental in seeing that Flotilla 13 was deployed along the Lebanese coast to mount hit-and-run attacks against retreating Palestinian units.

Fittingly, on the twenty-third anniversary of the raid against Green Island, the second naval commando veteran to assume a spot on the IDF General Staff and a man who had raised the standards of Israel's underwater warriors to an all-time and courageous high was named the IDF Navy commander. He was Amichai Eilon, a critically wounded hero from Green Island, a wounded hero from Tripoli, and a walking example of the miracle of medical science and the tenacious character of the human spirit. With a disability that would remove most professional soldiers from active duty assignments, Eilon continued to serve above and beyond the call of duty.

Eilon is one of the two men in the forty-six-year history of the IDF Navy to be awarded the I'tur Ha'Gvura bravery medal, a yellow ribbon that is Israel's highest award for valor and comparable to the American Medal of Honor and the British Victoria Cross; the other recipient, of course, was also a naval commando. Although the coveted I'tur Ha'Gvura was for Green Island, it could have been

for any one of a number of operations Eilon participated in or led throughout his illustrious thirty-year service. The Harvard-educated officer paid his dues throughout his rise up the IDF's ladder of command—serving in patrol boat squadrons, commanding missile boats, and even commanding the IDF Navy's two largest bases at Ashdod and Haifa. Yet his mark was on the naval commandos; it was to be a force where only the best would be allowed in, and their standards for combat would be the highest in the IDF. During Operation Peace for Galilee, for example, Colonel Eilon was involved in special operations in the north and personally guided Flotilla 13's counterterrorist operations all along the Lebanese coast.

Major General Eilon joined an IDF General Staff populated by special operations officers who, many say, represent the *new* IDF. Lt. Gen. Ehud Barak, chief of staff, is a former commander of Sayeret Mat'kal, Israel's most decorated soldier, and a man who wrote the manual for Israeli special operations; the deputy chief of staff, Maj. Gen. Amnon Shahak, is a former Sayeret Tzanhanim officer; the A'man director, Maj. Gen. Uri Saguy, is a former commander of Sayeret Golani; the officer commanding (OC) Southern Command, Maj. Gen. Matan Vilnai, is a former Sayeret Tzanhanim commander; the OC Central Command, Maj. Gen. Danny Yatom, is a former Sayeret Mat'kal officer; and the OC Northern Command, Maj. Gen. Yitzhak Mordechai, is a former commander of the paratroop brigade. It is a General Staff designed to execute and excel at special operations. It is a General Staff, and an OC IDF Navy, destined to use the maximum potential of the brave batmen of Flotilla 13.

It is almost certain that the naval commandos' next operation, if it hasn't already occurred, will gather no fanfare or publicity. Even though the October 1991 international media news that the unit had been despatched to the high seas in order to sink a North Korean freighter ferrying SCUD-C missiles to Syria was more bravado than fact, it did represent the utter deterrent power Israel's naval commandos enjoy. Their abilities are their calling card, their means of delivery is pure stealth, and the results of their operations are absolutely potent.

Chapter 4

Sayeret Golani: Flying Tigers

On a cool spring night in one of the *hottest* flash points on earth, three heavily armed Palestinian terrorists, members of the Iraqi-controlled Arab Liberation Front (ALF), crossed the Lebanese frontier into Israel. They cut through the formidable fence, evaded several IDF patrols, and managed to enter the protected grounds of Kibbutz Misgav Am, a historic agricultural settlement too

Assembled before their command and brigade flag, Sayeret Golani soldiers stand at attention before commencing combat exercises.

close for comfort to the chaos of Lebanon. The settlers along the border had become used to the occasional terrorist artillery attacks, the odd Katyusha rocket thrown in to make a political point, and the frequent attempt by terror squads to cross the border; most of the attempts, of course, had been terminated by IDF patrols. The terrorists were part of the landscape of the neighborhood, and many of the brave families living so close to a nation gone mad had gotten used to the troubles. Nothing, however, could prepare them for what was about to transpire. The terrorists' objective that night, April 6–7, 1980, was to seize the Kibbutz nursery and hold the several dozen infants sleeping there hostage in a desperate game of nerves with the State of Israel.

The sector of the fence separating Israel and Lebanon that had been breached had been the responsibility of the 1st Golani Infantry Brigade. The unit had responded to the electronic trip wire of the border being crossed but had not interdicted the terrorists upon their initial contact with the frontier fence; the unit's Bedouin trackers had failed to hunt the infiltrators down before they reached a civilian settlement. Golani units were the first to reach the scene, however, and they immediately surrounded the embattled building. News of the attack set off urgent alarms in IDF Headquarters in Tel Aviv, and the chief of staff, Lt. Gen. Rafael ("Raful") Eitan, himself a veteran of many counterterrorist operations, most behind enemy lines, took a chopper to the northern frontier to supervise the inevitable rescue assault. For everyone involved, it was clear that this was going to be a difficult night.

Crouching behind a stone fence a few meters outside the besieged nursery, peering through a pair of battered field glasses, was Capt. Gunni Harnick, the commander of Sayeret Golani, the reconnaissance commando element of the 1st Golani Infantry Brigade. Because of its proximity to the Kibbutz, Sayeret Golani was rushed into the fray to assume control of the rescue operation. The members of the unit were not prepared for a midnight operation, but terrorists usually didn't send out invitations.

Captain Harnick was an officer known for assuming decisive command under fire and never relinquishing the initiative to the enemy. Less than an hour after arriving at the scene, he fired a flare into the crimson-colored sky and led his rescue assault. The terrorists realized that an attempt to dislodge them from their position was approaching, and they immediately opened fire. Their fusillade formed a gauntlet of exploding projectiles; RPG rounds, warheads designed to penetrate over a foot of a tank's armor, were fired at the encroaching reconnaissance commandos.

The terrorists' fire proved to be too much for the Sayeret Golani commandos to overcome, and the rescue bid collapsed; one reconnaissance soldier was killed in the melee as he attempted to break through the nursery's main door. Pressure mounted as the terrorists threatened to kill all the children they were holding by daybreak.

Eventually, commandos from Sayeret Mat'kal arrived on the scene, and Sayeret Golani was forced to play a supporting role in the rescue operation. At dawn, the Israeli commandos struck. The terrorists gave as good as they got and proved formidable—fanatical—foes. The final rescue assault was successful, and all three terrorists were gunned down. A terrible price had been paid, how-

Capt. Reuven ("Ruvka") Eliaz, the Sayeret Golani commander, briefs his soldiers, all camouflaged in their lizard-pattern fatigues, prior to their epic battle at Tel Fahar at the end of the 1967 Six Day War. The conflict was one of the first true examples of Sayeret Golani's special talents as a special operations force.

Sayeret Golani commandos demonstrate their role in the rescue of a nursery at Kibbutz Misgav Am on April 7, 1980. Note the bullet-proof vests worn for the close-quarter melee.

ever. Two Golani had been killed in the nighttime bloodshed, as had one two-year-old girl, murdered by terrorist gunfire.

The attack on Misgav Am, like so many terrorist attacks before it, would not go unpunished. Revenge is the currency of life and death in the Middle East, and it is a motivator. It is also a deterrent. Fittingly, Sayeret Golani would be permitted to exact that much-coveted vengeance.

On the night of February 22, 1981, an IAF CH-53 Yasur chopper crossed the boundaries separating Israel and Lebanon and ferried a force of over a dozen Sayeret Golani commandos into the Nabatiyah Heights, into the center of bandit country, near the Christian town of el-Kfur, population 1,350 and regional headquarters to the ALF. Several Bell-212s, the miniworkhorses of the IAF's chopper fleet, landed Sayeret Golani ambush and cover forces around the town, and Force A, the attacking element, led by Capt. Gunni Harnick, commander of the unit, was to destroy the main ALF headquarters complex, which consisted of three one-story buildings spread out in a heavily fortified perimeter; it was a task the soldiers attended to with meticulous precision and the unforgiving devastation of a group of fighters obsessed with revenge. Against persistent hails of terrorist fire, the Sayeret Golani commandos, all burdened with extra loads of explosives and ammunition, managed to advance with speed and dexterity, overcoming obstacles and burning vehicles to kill ten terrorists and destroy their headquarters with a powerful load of high explosives. The raid, known as Operation New Technology, was carried out with brilliant success. Sayeret Golani would be back in Lebanon a little more than a year later. A year later, Harnick would be dead, killed in a bitter battle in a bitter war.

Being a member of one of the IDF's most capable elite units, especially being its commander, is a precarious existence.

The soldiers who wear Sayeret Golani's flying tiger wings over their left breast pocket and who proudly wear the brown beret are, indeed, a unique breed of fighter. They are not commandos in the true meaning of the word—they are not paratroopers, they are not part of a unit mandated to one specific task, and they are not as enigmatic as many other IDF commandos. After all, they are an intrinsic element of a conventional infantry brigade with little romance and even less mystery. Yet the members of Sayeret Golani can pride themselves in being truly special. Many senior IDF commanders consider the Flying Tigers to be the premier Sayeret in all of Israel. When a difficult operation needs to be executed, like the capture of a position held by Syrian commandos or the assassination of a terrorist chieftain, Sayeret Golani is called upon. It is, the *Dirty Harry* unit of the IDF. Whenever a difficult task that nobody else wants must be done, Sayeret Golani gets the call.

Throughout its forty-year-plus history, Sayeret Golani's flying tiger calling card dots the landscape of the Arab-Israeli campaign, from Rafah in the Sinai Desert to Nafekh atop the Golan Heights, from the squalor of the Gaza Strip to the desolate treachery of Fatahland, from the runway at Entebbe to the tarmac at Beirut International Airport.

The 1st Golani Infantry Brigade was one of the first truly conventional fighting formations conceived by the Haganah to defend against the expected Arab invasion once the Jewish State declared its independence; when the IDF was formally created in June 1948, the brigade became the Army's defensive—and offensive—cornerstone. Despite chronic shortages of weapons and training facilities, the brigade fought effectively in

On June 7, 1982, battered by time and the ferocious battle between Palestinian gunmen and Sayeret Golani waged only hours earlier, Beaufort Castle stands stoically in the distance as the last remnants of the Flying Tigers prepare to board a Bell-212 chopper back to Israel and the funerals of seven of their comrades.

the conquest of Tiberias and Safed, as well as the extremely bloody defense of Kibbutz Kfar Szold and Tirat Zvi in Galilee. Toward the end of the 1948 fighting, the Golani Brigade was shipped south, toward the Negev Desert and the conquest of the Port of Aqaba town of Eilat. Soon, however, the brigade would earn itself a negative reputation because it was transformed into a national melting pot for immigrants from over sixty nations. Many of these newcomers to the newly established Jewish State were poor and desperate, and some even sold their unit's combat boots to pay for food for their families languishing in transit camps. Yet the brigade had a shining spot: a small, rogue, and extremely capable reconnaissance platoon, known as Ha'Machleket Ha'Kommando, or Commando Platoon, also known as the Machleket Siyur Meyuchedet, or Special Reconnaissance Platoon, led by the rogue warrior Rafi Kotzer.

The Golani commandos were not as glamorous as the Pal'mach, but their exploits behind

A Sayeret Golani commando demonstrates firing his Glilon 5.56mm SAR equipped with a laser aiming device. The Flying Tigers deployed their night-fighting capabilities brilliantly during the unit's epic raid against Ahmed Jibril's PFLP-GC headquarters at al-Na'ameh on December 8–9, 1988. IT Lasers

enemy lines and raiding of Syrian staging areas earned them an everlasting reputation of combat effectiveness. An early commander of this Golani reconnaissance element was a young lieutenant named Ariel ("Arik") Sharon, who commanded what would become known as Sayeret Golani in 1951; needless to say, Sharon's influence on Sayeret Golani, as well as the entire gamut of Israeli special operations, was profound. To increase unit morale and make its distinction as a combat force evident, the commandos adopted the nickname Ha'Namer Ha'Me'ufaf, or Flying Tiger; a small flying tiger made of silver metal became the unit badge, worn proudly on the chest of each reconnaissance commando. Because the Hebrew word *Namer* can mean both Tiger and Leopard, the actual English-translation to Sayeret Golani's nickname has been the source of some mystery; on numerous occasions, including previous books by this author, the name Flying Leopards was used. It is now understood that the *accurate* title of the unit is, indeed, the Flying Tigers.

For the next fifteen years, Sayeret Golani slowly built a reputation for itself as a premier IDF reconnaissance formation. When Unit 101 and Sayeret Tzanhanim were grabbing all the headlines and taking care of the difficult combat assignments and counterterrorist operations behind enemy lines, Sayeret Golani was hard at work consolidating its unique family of fighters, and that meant operations against the Syrians. The two Sayeret Golani operations that stand out for their daring and explosive manner are Operation Cricket, on the night of February 1, 1960, when a force from Sayeret Golani attacked Syrian gun positions at Tewfiq, just below the volcanic cliffs of the Golan Heights, and Operation Swallow, the March 16–17, 1962, Golani raid against the Syrian gun positions at Nuqieb, on the shores of the Sea of Galilee, a few kilometers from the Israeli frontier.

What made Sayeret Golani special in these early years was the decisive leadership of its commanders. These officers led their soldiers by example, and *only* by example. The fighters were only as good as their commander, and the commander was supposed to be second to none. As a result of this tremendous burden of command and responsibility to the members of the unit, many

Sayeret Golani commanders would fall in the line of duty in the years to follow. Self-sacrifice, like the symbol of the flying tiger, would also become a Sayeret Golani calling card.

On June 9, 1967, as the Six Day War was nearing its abrupt end, Israel headed north toward the treacherous Golan Heights. For years, Syrian artillery emplacements atop the impregnable Golan Heights had harassed Israeli Kibbutzim and Moshavim with incessant and deadly barrages; Israeli retaliatory air strikes and commando raids never managed to silence the menacing guns. Now, with the Sinai Desert in Israeli hands, Egypt thrashed on the battlefield, and Jerusalem liberated by Israeli paratroopers, the full attention of

the IDF could finally be diverted to Syria and, most important, the capture of the Golan Heights as a threat to its north. The Golan Heights was protected by a series of forts that dominated the steep approaches with dozens of gun emplacements and machine gun positions; they were gauntlets of destruction that promised to turn any Israeli assault into a massacre. Israel, however, could no longer leave the heights in Syrian hands and allow its citizens to be subjected to the murderous artillery attacks. On June 9, the IDF struck. One of the first Syrian positions to be hit was also one of the most strategic. It was Tel Fahar, and it would become a key entry in the Sayeret Golani battle log in much the same way that El Alamein would en-

"Advance and fire. . . . Advance and fire!" A Sayeret Golani is acclimated with the combat reality of fighting on the Golan Heights, during exercises near the Syrian frontier, as he lays another five-round burst of 5.56mm fire into another target.

dear the British Eighth Army to the world and Iwo Jima would come to personify the very fiber of the U.S. Marine Corps.

The unit originally tasked with neutralizing Tel Fahar, the Monster, was the Golani Brigade's Barak, or Lightning, Battalion, but it suffered horrific casualties in its initial assault; many infantry soldiers had been killed in the close-quarter melee, including battalion commander Lt. Col. Mussa Klein. To keep a deteriorating situation from developing into a blood bath, the brigade's Sayeret was called in.

Commanded by Capt. Reuven ("Ruvka") Eliaz, Sayerct Golani entered the battle at a time when the Barak Battalion was close to being decimated and the Syrians were assuming a lethal offensive initiative. The situation changed dramat-

ically when Captain Eliaz appeared with his commandos, adorned in lizard-pattern camouflage fatigues. Around his cry of "Follow me!" Captain Eliaz rallied his soldiers in a thunderous barrage of unrelenting submachine fire. The subsequent fighting was fierce. Commandos who ran out of ammunition picked up the weapons of fallen comrades; once these weapons would no longer fire, they were used as truncheons. Fists replaced side arms, and bazookas were used at pointblank range. Inside underground bunkers and communications trenches, commandos and Syrian soldiers fought to the death in dozens of private battles. The devastation was absolute, but in the end, Sayeret Golani persevered.

On the morning of June 10, Israeli helicopters landed atop the peak of Mt. Hermon—the region's

Loaded down with weaponry and equipment, a team of Sayeret Golani grenadiers negotiates the rocky and *inhospitable terrain of northern Israel during assault training.*

dominant mountain connecting Lebanon and Syria and affectionately known in Arabic as Jebel es-Sheikh, or the Old Man, for its snow-capped peaks—to complete Israel's capture of the Golan Heights. It was a strategic bit of real estate, looking straight into the Syrian heartland, and had been a source of Arab pride for centuries. The Star of David flying atop the majestic peak was a reflection as much of the Israeli victory as of the Syrian defeat—one Syria vowed to avenge.

In late October 1973, the 1st Golani Infantry Brigade was supposed to have conducted its twenty-fifth anniversary celebration in Tel Aviv's Hayarkon Park. Golani veterans from each of Israel's wars were to have gathered in an emotional reverence to their fallen, scarred, and surviving comrades-in-arms. Most important, however, the anniversary was to initiate a new era for the Golani Infantry Brigade and its esteemed Sayeret. Following four major wars and countless retaliatory raids against enemy positions and operations along Israel's precarious frontiers, the brigade was to enter into its second quarter century of military responsibility to Israel's north stronger and better equipped than ever before.

Between 1967 and 1973, Golani's responsibility to northern Israel had been paid in blood. In the rolling, desolate hills of southern Lebanon, near the Syrian frontier, units from the brigade led by Sayeret Golani fought an unforgiving counterinsurgency campaign against Palestinian terrorists on a battlefield known as Fatahland. Few units could have waged such a difficult and bloody war of nerves in such terrain—mountains peppered with endless caves, brutally hot in the summer and arctic cold in the winter—and against a terrorist army determined on martyring itself for the liberation of its Palestinian homeland from the Jews. Few units other than Sayeret Golani could have persisted. Yet Tel Fahar, Fatahland, and everything else aside, on Yom Kippur Day, October 6, 1973, Golani's worth as a unit, as well as its very existence, was put to the test.

The Syrian surprise attack against the Golan Heights at 1340 hours on October 6 was the culmination of what to many was blatantly obvious. On September 13, 1973, twelve Syrian Air Force MiG-21s were blown out of the skies above Latakia by a flight of IAF warplanes over the Mediterranean. The Syrians replied to this humiliating aerial mauling by mobilizing their armed forces along the Purple Line, the border between Israeli and Syrian forces along the Golan Heights—a move that promised full-scale war. The failure of IDF Military Intelligence to realize that the Syrian build-up was in full coordination with identical Egyptian moves along the Suez Canal prohibited sufficient Israeli defensive—or preemptive offensive—responses from being implemented.

The IDF military formation responsible for defending the Golan Heights was Ugdat Raful, a mixed armored and mechanized infantry division task force commanded by Brig. Gen. Rafael ("Raful") Eitan, the IDF's chief of staff during the 1982 War in Lebanon. Ugdat Raful boasted impressive armor capabilities—the efficient 188th Barak Brigade under Col. Yitzhak Ben-Shoham's leadership and rambunctious Col. Avigdor ("Yanush") Ben-Gal's elite 7th Armored Brigade being the vanguard of this might. In fact, the epic tank battles that resulted in the destruction of the 188th Brigade and the 7th Brigade's legendary defense of the Valley of Tears have come to characterize the war on the Golan Heights in 1973. The bitter battles atop the volcanic Golan plateau were also marked by the heroic and stoic effort of Ugdat Raful's primary infantry force: the Golani Brigade.

On October 6, the only Golani unit positioned between the Syrian border and the Israeli heartland was the Gideon Battalion, which was thinly spread out along the series of seventeen Mutzavim, or fortifications, along the Purple Line from Mt. Hermon to the Jordanian border, even though the only position to fall on the Golan Heights was Mutzav 104, the electronic intelligence-gathering post atop Mt. Hermon. Although defended by a mere thirteen Golani NCOs, as well as forty-one electronic and intelligence noncombatant specialists, the position was known as the eyes and ears of the nation and considered a sensitive target. It was, however, seized by a determined heliborne force from the Syrian 82nd Paratroop Regiment, which easily outnumbered the position's Golani defenders. In the first moments of the conflict, Mutzav 104 was pounded by a massive Syrian artillery bombardment, the incoming shells providing cover for four Mi-8 Hip helicopters, which attempted to land on the Israeli peak. One Mi-8 was hit by .50cal fire and exploded into a fiery ball in midair, but the others soon landed and, after securing a momentary landing zone, swiftly disgorged dozens of heavily armed commandos wearing intimidating lizard-pattern camouflage fatigues. The Syrian paratroopers quickly seized the initiative against the lightly armed Golani garrison and secured the position's outer perimeter. Forced into the complex's maze of underground bunkers, control rooms, and barracks, Mt. Hermon's defenders soon found themselves cut off, isolated, and desperately short on time and ammunition. Many surrendered; others ran off into the night to try to reach friendly lines. Only eleven of the twenty who set out survived the despondent attempt to reach "safe lines"; their tales of the Syrian special forces onslaught became a rallying point for Israeli resolve in the remainder of the conflict.

On the morning of October 7, Col. Amir Drori, commander of the brigade, gazed toward the Mt.

Having fought in the trenches in Tel Fahar, atop Mt. Hermon, and in Lebanon atop Beaufort Castle and underneath al-Na'ameh, Sayeret Golani commandos master trench warfare amid a cloud of dust and the engulfing stench of cordite in the Negev Desert.

Hermon position from his perch at Ugdat Raful headquarters at Nafekh and vowed revenge. Mt. Hermon would be retaken, even though the brigade's first attempt to recapture the strategic summit, headed by the Flying Tigers, ended in failure. Led by Capt. Shmaryahu Vinnik, commander of the unit, commandos from Sayeret Golani spearheaded the two-battalion assault up the daunting cliffs. The Golani attack force, together with two supporting Centurion tanks, began their ascent sticking to the main road, while Sayeret Golani commandos fanned out along the rocky embankment, attempting to provide the mechanized elements with a precariously thin, though present, cover force. As the advance continued its dogged pace, Syrian paratroopers suddenly appeared from behind dozens of large boulders and dug-in firing positions; snipers with 7.62mm Drugenov rifles exacted a heavy toll on the surrounded and cutoff Sayeret Golani fighters—especially among officers and squad leaders. The Sayeret advanced quickly and engaged the Syrians in hand-to-hand fighting. Shouting in Arabic and Hebrew, commandos from two armies fought it out with fists, rocks, and knives; their screams were heard over the incessant gunfire. The "second" battle for Mt. Hermon was a fierce display of the brigade's resolve but in the end, failed to dislodge the Syrians from one centimeter of territory.

For the next thirteen days of the conflict, Mt. Hermon remained a thorn in Israel's backside. By October 21, with the IDF deep inside Syria and a United Nations–imposed cease-fire imminent, the time to retake Mt. Hermon was at hand and precariously ticking away. In coordination with heavy air and artillery support, the Golani Brigade was to assault the mountain at night, while a two-company-size force of approximately 300 paratroopers would land by helicopter on the "Syrian" peak of Mt. Hermon and support the Golani assault. The assault was code named Operation Kinuach, or Dessert—the closing course to a bitter war. While the remainder of the brigade made its slow and deliberate advance up the steep cliffs, Sayeret Golani would advance ahead of all the other forces.

At 2000 hours, the ascent up the steep cliffs of Mt. Hermon began. The Golani fighters all carried extra loads of ammunition, as they expected a hellish, almost suicidal, fight. The night's inky darkness provided the advance ample cover from the Syrian guns but made the climb a difficult and frightening experience. The ascent lasted 6 full hours until, at 0200 hours on October 22, the nighttime's silence was shattered with the sound of automatic fire. The third battle for Mt. Hermon was underway. Green tracer lines suddenly illuminated the pitch black autumn sky, as thousands of bullets began to concentrate on the Golani fighters racing for cover. Syrian mortar and RPG fire was called in, and, within moments, casualties began to reach catastrophic levels; the desperate cries for medics were heard even over the gunfire as medical orderlies soon became the brigade's most valued asset.

Originally, the capture of the strategic cable car area was given to Golani's Habok'im Ha'Rishonim, or First Conquerors, Battalion, but it encountered severe Syrian opposition, and the mission eventually fell to the Flying Tigers, who had their hands full with other responsibilities. Under Captain Vinnik's unrelenting command, the Sayeret reached its objective without incident. But the initial patrols despatched to map out the situation discovered a serious Syrian military presence in the area, and a pitched battle developed.

As is often the tragic case of combat commanders in the IDF, the officer was the first to get hit by enemy fire. A Syrian paratrooper who had jumped out from behind a massive volcanic boulder firing his AK-47 assault rifle hit Captain Vinnik before Sayeret Golani commandos could return fire. Although bleeding profusely, Captain Vinnik continued to issue orders and to direct his fighters in the developing battle. Attempts to rescue the Sayeret commander met with failure; Syrian fire did not discriminate between combatants and healers, and many medics were cut down as well by accurate bursts from well-entrenched machine guns.

The Sayeret managed to secure a firebase for itself, and with the assistance of rifle-grenade fire and RPGs taken from dead Syrian soldiers, the unit neutralized the Syrian resistance to the thuds of occasional sniper fire. At 0730 hours, the Syrians began fleeing their positions and surrendering to the exhausted commandos of the Sayeret. Captain

A Sayeret Golani sniper team, the marksman equipped with an M-21, deploys atop a dominating peak, ready for action. Being a sniper in the IDF's special forces is a precarious and much-sought-after profession.

Vinnik was brought down the mountain by stretcher, although he died hours later from his massive wounds. His dying words, according to comrades, were, "We must never descend from the Hermon." He was posthumously given the rank of major and awarded the I'tur Ha'Mofet medal of valor, or Distinguished Service Medal.

For the next 5 hours, the battle raged, until finally, at 1100 hours, the Israeli and Golani flags were hoisted atop the listening post's chief antenna. Moments later, Golani communications officers announced the historic "Calling all stations. . . . Mt. Hermon is in our hands."

The 9-hour battle had turned the once-peaceful mountain into a hill of blood and mangled flesh.

Fifty-five Golani fighters were killed that October morning, and seventy-nine wounded. The recapture of Mt. Hermon was the Golani Brigade's finest hour and its costliest hour. During the 1973 Yom Kippur War's eighteen days of combat, the Golani Brigade lost 130 dead and 310 wounded. In keeping with the IDF elite unit ethic of "Follow me," the greatest casualties were endured among the senior officers. The brigade lost Lt. Col. Reuven ("Ruvka") Eliaz, its deputy commander and former Sayeret leader, as well as Maj. Shmaryahu Vinnik, its Sayeret commander, and countless platoon and squad leaders. Although devastated, leaderless, and in disarray, the Golani Brigade was not through in its duties atop Mt. Hermon.

Hell Town and built-up area combat training, Sayeret Golani style. A Sayeret Golani second lieutenant guides his FN MAG gunner as an enemy fortification is attended to.

A bitter war of attrition followed the October 24 cease-fire agreement; Syrian commando forces —with help from a Cuban expeditionary force of sorts—made several determined and courageous attempts to once again recapture Mt. Hermon. This time, however, the Golani defenders, mainly the fighters who wore the flying tiger across their chest, remained undaunted. They stood their ground and reaffirmed their role as a special operations infantry force by pushing back any attempt to infiltrate into Israeli lines that had been fought for with dire determination and paid for with blood and fallen comrades. The war atop Mt. Hermon, especially in the deep snows of the winter of 1973–74, was particularly fierce and brutal; it

was a conflict where a commando dagger placed into the back of a sentry and a lone shot from a sniper were the order of the day. Sayeret Golani was also bloodied during this time period, in keeping true to its role as a guardian of Israel's north—a role terrorist infiltrations and full-scale combat in Lebanon would severely test years later.

By retrieving Israel's "eyes and ears" during the 1973 War, Sayeret Golani endeared itself as a premier IDF fighting unit. By assaulting a block of flats held by terrorists from Ahmed Jibril's PFLP-General Command on April 11, 1974, in the northern town of Qiryat Shmoneh, Sayeret Golani became an intrinsic element of the day-to-day security of the residents of northern Israel. Yet, it

With kneepads firmly in place and his back thrown against a bullet-riddled wall, a Sayeret Golani trooper quickly reloads his Galil with a fresh new magazine.

75

was its participation in a unique rescue operation, in the heart of Africa, that earned the Sayeret, as well as the remainder of the brigade, the honor of being a Yechida Muvcheret, or Chosen Unit, the IDF's term for special forces unit, which it had worked for nearly thirty years to achieve.

Sayeret Golani was one of the units chosen by Brig. Gen. Dan Shomron, chief paratroop and infantry officer, to participate in the July 3–4, 1976, Operation Thunderball rescue at Entebbe. The Sayeret Golani contingent, led by Col. Uri Saguy—commander of the brigade, former commander of Sayeret Golani during the dark days of the Fatah-land campaign, and future director of A'man—was responsible for securing the Sayeret Mat'kal res-

cue of the hostages in the terminal building and destroying Idi Amin's air force so that an aerial pursuit of the IAF C-130s could not be mounted. Equipped with armored personnel carriers and RPG antitank weapons as well as .50cal machine guns, the Sayeret Golani commandos destroyed dozens of Ugandan MiG combat aircraft as they sat in their tarmac parking spots. For Sayeret Golani's participation in Operation Thunderball, the entire Golani Brigade was allowed the unique distinction of wearing the unit's own brown beret.

On June 6, 1982, the IDF invaded Lebanon in what became known as Operation Peace for Galilee. One of the first objectives of the IDF advance was the neutralization of the old crusader fortress

"So you want to purify an enemy stronghold?" A Sayeret Golani sergeant guides a fellow trooper through an urban nightmare obstacle course during

La'Ba'B training, early in the commandos' course of instruction.

Beaufort Castle, known by the IDF as the Monster—an ancient facility that had been used for a long time by the Palestinians, and Syrian intelligence, as an artillery observation post for directing fire into northern Israel; almost the whole of the northern Galilee region could be seen from this 717m-high perch. For years before the Israeli invasion, the capture of the Monster had been entrusted to Sayeret Golani. The unit had planned its eventual seizure, studied intelligence films on the fortress's layout, and trained to fight a close-quarter battle after climbing up treacherous heights and being fired upon by well-entrenched defenders. The position atop this ancient relic of the region's penchant for war was reinforced by deep trenches, bunkers, and fortified passageways surrounded by 3.65m-thick walls that were impervious to most conventional explosives. The crusaders had built their stronghold well, and now it was in the hands of el-Fatah special operations units.

The original plan called for the Sayeret, supported by units from Pal'Han Golani, or Golani Engineering Company, the brigade's engineer and sapper force, to attack at 1100 hours, but traffic jams of tanks and armored personnel carriers (APCs) led to a 7-hour delay. As a result, the Sayeret Golani task force, commanded by Maj. Gunni Harnick, was compelled to attack at the onset of darkness. At H-hour plus 7, Major Harnick assembled his soldiers for action. They leapt off their M113 APC at the base of the mountain and began their precarious assault in a mad dash of war cries and full automatic bursts of fire. The Palestinians opened fire immediately, and a pitched battle developed as the commandos, supported by limited artillery cover, commenced their ascension.

In meticulous fashion, the Sayeret Golani commandos purified each Palestinian bunker by tossing in a grenade and then raking the firing position with decimating automatic bursts of fire. Many of the el-Fatah terrorists fled at the onset of the attack, but many opted to fight to the death. Hand-to-hand battles ensued, as did countless knife fights, fistfights, and gunfights using Glilon 5.56mm SARs at pointblank "head banger" range. LAW rockets, 66mm rockets for destroying tanks, were used in an antipersonnel role. The combat was so fierce that the Flying Tigers were forced to strip the Palestinian dead of their AK-47s, Drugenovs, and RPKs when they ran out of ammunition for their own Galils and FN MAGs. The fighting lasted a full 6 nonstop hours, and the battle still raged with unrelenting ferocity—already, several commandos had been killed, and over a dozen more seriously wounded. Yet, before Harnick could lead his fighters to overcome the final Palestinian bunker, he was struck in the chest by a burst of Palestinian machine gun fire as he led a charge. He was killed instantly, and his deputy, 1st Lt. Mordechai Goldman, took his place, throwing a satchel charge into the bunker that had launched the murderous volley at his beloved commander. The bunker erupted into a fireball and collapsed in a cloud of debris. Finally, the Israeli flag was hoisted above the Monster.

The next day, under great pomp and ceremony, Prime Minister Menachem Begin and Defense Minister Arik Sharon, both of Israel, formally handed over control of the Monster to renegade major Sa'ad Haddad of Lebanon, in a symbolic ending to PLO domination over southern Lebanon and northern Israel. The commandos of Sayeret Golani were in no mood to celebrate, however. They had lost six of their own, as well as their commander.

During the course of the war, Sayeret Golani participated in dozens of special operations, including the attack on Jebel Barouk, a top-secret Syrian signal intelligence (SIGINT) position in the Beka'a Valley, and the capture of Beirut International Airport. In the subsequent years of Israel's staged withdrawal from southern Lebanon and deadly battles against Shi'ite guerrillas, Sayeret Golani played an instrumental role in hitting terrorist targets with preemptive destruction before they could attack Israeli forces. Sayeret Golani's mark in southern Lebanon will not soon be forgotten.

What makes the members of Sayeret Golani special? Why is theirs a premier reconnaissance unit? Why are they the IDF's best conventional commandos?

Unlike other elite Israeli combat reconnaissance fighters, the commandos of Sayeret Golani are not chosen from a crop of raw recruits at Ba'Ku'M. "This is the paratroopers' way of doing things, not ours," said Captain D., a Sayeret Golani officer. Before the brigade will even consider soldiers for a spot in the Sayeret, they must first prove their worth as regular infantry soldiers in the parent brigade—which is no small feat. They undergo basic infantry training and survive the mud and cold of field instruction, endless hours of weapons training, and the other indignities of "basic." From the time Golani soldiers leave Ba'Ku'M with their kitbag in hand to the time, following a forced march or two, that they place the yellow and green unit tag across their epaulet, the infantry soldiers are monitored for leadership qualities, combat skills, and other "intangibles," such as charisma, intelligence, and the ability to rally fighters around them. The soldiers who display these skills are usually predesignated as officer material and, following several months of distinguished service, are sent to officer's course. The infantry soldiers who display these skills with abundance are offered the treasured opportunity

to volunteer into the brigade's Sayeret. Sayeret Golani will only accept the very best the brigade has to offer. This standard of excellence separates the unit from most of the other Sayerot or commando units in the IDF's order of battle—and it has made Sayeret Golani truly the IDF's best.

The invitation to volunteer into the Sayeret is just that: an invitation. Nothing more. Before the eager foot-slogging infantry soldiers can begin their Sayeret training, they must prove that they are worthy of wearing the flying tiger wings and worthy of receiving the expensive Sayeret Golani training. Before anything can happen, they must undergo a Gibush. The fun has only just begun.

Unlike other Gibushim, this one is attended to without the innocence of soldiers in the Army for a full 5 hours. Beyond the grueling physical examinations, the Gibush also requires proving one's combat skills. Golani infantry soldiers might be able to do 100 sit-ups without respite and overcome an obstacle course without breaking a sweat, but if they can't hit a target on the first ten shots, they will never make it as members of this exclusive unit. On the other hand, the soldiers could be crack shots; their hits on the range can be bunched up with virtually little separation, but if they lack some physical distinction and endurance, they, too, will not become members of the Sayeret Golani. It is, indeed, unique that a group of NCOs, including corporals and sergeants, must battle one another to obtain a coveted spot on the Sayeret Golani roster, but the brigade views this competition with great affection. After all, it has helped put its Sayeret a cut above just about every other one for virtually three decades.

Failing the Gibush provides disappointed infantrymen with a bus ticket back to their battalion, but for those who pass the Gibush, nothing is guaranteed. Everything starts again. New training, new rigors, new limits placed on a soldier's endurance. The true length of the actual Sayeret Golani training is classified, as is the exact itinerary of instruction. According to foreign reports, Sayeret Golani instruction includes proficiency in every weapon to be found in the area, cold-killing, demolitions, parachuting, escape and evasion, survival, heliborne infiltration and exfiltration techniques, and intelligence work.

"Kadima. . . . Acharai!"—"Forward. . . . Follow me!" A force of Sayeret Golani commandos emerges from its hiding position atop a hill and launches a surprise attack against a "fortified" position during maneuvers in northern Israel.

One known aspect of the Flying Tigers training is Hell Town.

Hell Town is a small city of concrete huts, bunkers, and alleyways meant to reproduce the physical characteristics of a small urban center. The training facility earns its ominous name by being assaulted virtually every week of the year with thousands of tons of ordnance, high explosives and other assorted tools of war and destruction. It is where the Israeli infantrymen or paratrooper learns the art of La'Ba'B, the Hebrew acronym for *Lechima Be'Shetach Banu'i*, or Built-up Area Combat, one of the most crucial aspects of special operations taught by the IDF. In the first few days of a chilly week in March, Hell Town belongs to Sayeret Golani. The objective of this close-quarter training is clear: to teach the recon-naissance commando the proper physical techniques required to lurch around buildings, corners, and alleyways, as well as the proper methods of using one's personal assault weapon. Obviously, a soldier will use a grenade or rocket launcher quite differently in the open plains of Galilee than he would inside a Beirut apartment block, and this art of split-second precision when pulling a trigger, or hurling a grenade into a room *must* be mastered if the target is to be captured with the minimal of Israeli casualties. Operation Peace for Galilee proved that Sayeret Golani possessed the skills to capture a built-up area. Hell Town was meant to ensure that future targets would be seized before the enemy knew what hit it.

Today's practice is relatively simple: three concrete houses, complete with steel shutters over

Alpinistim winter warriors evacuate a "wounded" comrade during maneuvers atop Mt. Hermon. The CAR-15 5.56mm assault rifles fitted with sniper scopes and indigenously produced white winter gear are unique for an army used to fighting in the desert!

nonexistent windows and steel doors, must be purified of an enemy presence by a single squad. The buildings, ostensibly, are terrorist headquarters and need to be captured intact so that "valuable" intelligence material inside can be taken back to Israel for analysis. Two dummies— store mannequins found in a Tel Aviv junkyard— dressed in lizard-pattern camouflage fatigues and Kefiyeh headdresses stand on top of the one-story buildings as sentries. Obviously, they need to be removed first, and two snipers are given that task.

Since it is dusk, and an eerie crimson cloud has engulfed the training facility, the first sniper, Sergeant Rami, will rely on a Galil assault rifle fitted with a laser sighting device; it shines its thin red beam onto the point of the target that will be struck. Naturally, the laser beam is aimed at the "terrorist's" head. The second sniper, Corporal Yossi, is armed with an M-21 sniper's rifle, a sturdy piece of death that could hit almost any target in its maximum 700m range. They are both in the prone position, fatigue caps turned around so that the brim will not interfere with the operation of their weapons. Corporal Rami wears a camouflaged cap, adorned with a U.S. woodland pattern, that he purchased from a Jerusalem survival store; to make it "semiofficial," his girlfriend has painted the flying tiger emblem over the front with some red nail polish. Over both snipers stands the unit marksmanship officer, Second Lieutenant R. Ac-

Alpinistim commandos, all heavily armed and ready to commence their combat assault maneuvers in the snowy depths, assemble into their respective teams.

cording to the popular scuttlebutt permeating through the Sayeret Golani ranks, First Lieutenant R. is capable of hitting a fly languishing on a mound of cow chips at a range of 45m with his 9mm pistol. It is impossible to tell if this is true or not, but R.'s reputation as a crack shot is legendary, as is Sayeret Golani's marksmanship. The unit's snipers —armed with M-21s, Galils, and M-16s fitted with a wide assortment of scopes—are among the best in Israel.

H-hour is set for 1755. The squads will begin their run to the three buildings a few moments before so that the sentries atop the roof can be eliminated at a point before they would discover the main force as it maneuvered in open ground, and late enough so that the sounds of the gunfire would not be able to forewarn the terrorists inside. At 1755 *exactly*, both snipers, already exhaling slowly, press their trigger mechanisms ever so gently and squeeze off one shot apiece. Naturally, both targets are hit in the head. The squad of Sayeret Golani commandos, split into three forces, race up against the outer walls of the three buildings, place the protective goggles strapped to their helmets over their eyes, and prepare their assault weapons for action; several of the commandos are equipped with nonconventional IDF weapons, including the Israel Military Industries Timberwolf shotguns, and the new Negev 5.56mm light machine gun. Trailing behind the Sayeret Golani squad is Major I., the Sayeret commander, armed with a stopwatch and a bullhorn.

A Sayeret Golani squad, its commanders nervously clutching their specially modified Glilon SARs, checks back with headquarters before pursuing suspicious movements in the southern Lebanon security zone.

The three forces all line up against the building with their backs against the wall. Each fighter clutches a Glilon SAR gingerly, as they know they will soon be asked to burst into a darkened room and pepper it with accurate bursts of automatic fire. The lead commando clutches his Glilon with his right hand and holds a Mk. 26 antipersonnel fragmentation grenade in his left hand. At the signal of the force commander, he swings open the door, pulls the pin from the grenade, yells "Rimon," or "Grenade," at the top of his lungs, and gently tosses the grenade inside the first room. All the commandos suddenly crouch down and prepare to get their legs in motion. The grenade detonates in a thunderous blast, and the fragments can be heard bouncing off the walls, which are reinforced with special materials to prevent injury to the troopers undergoing training; this is the signal to move in. The lead trooper holds the door open, and his comrades race inside, each one firing in a different direction, each one careful to avoid hitting a fellow soldier. The illuminated rounds and tracer fire inside the darkened room look like the electronic flashes of a video game; the crackling explosions of automatic gunfire are deafening and cause some of the commandos to think what it must be like to sit inside a tin can after someone has tossed a firecracker in. These live-fire assaults are mesmerizing. They are also dangerous. Second Lieutenant Rafi, a two-year

A Sayeret Golani officer and his radioman—whose helmet graffiti seem to indicate he has other plans with his time—scan across the Lebanese border during patrol duty.

veteran of the Sayeret, said: "La'Ba'B is like walking on red hot coals. You have to know how to do it, and you have to know how not to get burned!"

Entering the building is only the beginning of the exercise. After everything is secure and the brigade command post has been informed of the mission's success, an ammunition dump and several vehicles (former Egyptian army BTR-152s) are attended to with equal destruction. Three commandos—one armed with an RPG, one armed with an LAW, and one equipped with antitank rifle grenades—race to an adjacent field. They spread out, launch themselves into a prone firing position, pull their trigger, and fire. The sounds of antitank projectiles is deafening but nothing when compared with the sound of their impact into the center of their target and the heat of the fireballs emanating from the destroyed target.

Major I. is pleased with the results but not fully satisfied. The Sayeret Golani commander realizes that no aspect in the Sayeret Golani vocabulary is as important as built-up area fighting. A veteran of many Sayeret Golani operations behind enemy lines, including the bloody al-Na'ameh raid against Ahmed Jibril and the PFLP-GC near Beirut, Major I. knows how treacherous even the safe confines of an urban obstacle course can be, but he also realizes that Hell Town is a picnic when compared with the real thing. The soldiers will continue to train.

From Hell Town, the Sayeret Golani commandos head out to the open field to eat a "hell dinner": field rations and some tea. Their day, already 10 hours long and still ticking, will continue throughout the night. When it is pitch dark, the commandos will assault Hell Town with infrared goggles, laser targeting devices, and other secretive night-fighting bits of equipment. The illumination from dozens of laser beams and then ricocheting bits of shrapnel and spent tracer rounds will make a scene from *Star Wars* seem as dull a light show as that of a refrigerator light bulb.

To the commandos of Sayeret Golani, Hell Town will eventually be replaced by another type of hell: service along the Lebanese frontier and inside the security zone in southern Lebanon. It is a dirty, disgusting counterguerrilla campaign, yet they know that it is just the type of war for which

they have been trained. Ordered across the boundaries of the security zone to ambush terrorists eager to die in battle, the soldiers of Sayeret Golani must use all of their talents and skills to equalize the odds against them in a dangerous foreign land, where bloodshed and destruction are permanent fixtures of its landscape.

The Golani Brigade contains other "elite" units—including the engineering force Pal'han Golani and the brigade's Plugat Orev, or Crow's Company, which is also known in many circles, according to foreign reports, as Sayeret Orev, or Crow's Recon.

A footnote: During the bitter war of attrition that followed the 1973 War amid the snow-capped peaks of Mt. Hermon, the need to create a special force of snow warriors became accutely apparent to many IDF commanders—especially to Golani officers responsible for security in the north. Yet, it was only after Israel's involvement in Lebanon,

With a white Kefiyeh wrapped around his neck as a good luck symbol, a Sayeret Golani grenadier deploys with a modified Ma'Ga'Ch-7 tank in the rolling hills of northern Israel. Although a commando force, Sayeret Golani is not separate from the parent brigade and must operate as a conventional spearhead in operational assignments.

Back to basic: a Sayeret Golani team prepares to board its aerial taxi for the evening's activities in the security zone of southern Lebanon.

when the IDF experienced its first Lebanese winter, that the need to create a new alpine-type unit was propelled past official channels and finally materialized. It was a special force of commandos—mostly reservists, primarily former members of Sayeret Golani—specially trained to fight in the snow and difficult winter conditions. These Israeli snowfighters would become known as Ha'Alpinistim, or the Alpine Soldiers. In Mt. Hermon, an Alp-like peak close to the very soul of the Golani Brigade, the Alpinistim would have a natural training ground at their disposal for several months of the year; this elite IDF alpine unit is truly unique in that it must wait until the harsh weather of winter before it can be mobilized and then rushed into training.

Oddly enough, Mt. Hermon is a popular ski resort for many Israelis—it is the *only* ski resort in Israel!—and naturally, skiing is a mandatory skill for all the commandos in the unit. To make sure these soldiers-of-the-desert and part-time winter commandos don't lose their special snow skills, special ski instructors are brought into their training periods to allow them the opportunity to become cross-country fighting machines. The

deep snows and occasional blizzard conditions usually found atop Mt. Hermon make it ideal for the Alpinistim to use the volatile piece of mountaintop real estate as their principal location for maneuvers; in fact, should Syria ever invade the Golan Heights in winter, this is where the Alpinistim will more than likely be bloodied.

Usually, the Alpinistim spend their time in the snow above Mt. Hermon executing survival training exercises. On one cool winter's day when, from the peak, the suburbs of Damascus can be seen, the Alpinistim unit is carried to the top of the mountain on the cable car that, during the weekend, ferries Israeli skiers to the mountain's highest perch. The fighters all wear a special white snowsuit, Hermonit winter boots, special sunglasses, and their white wool winter cap. Each commando carries a CAR-15 5.56mm assault rifle with a sniper's scope, and two of the commandos are carrying a sled with a wounded comrade packed comfortably inside. Removing a comrade, either hurt by the bitter cold elements or shot by a Syrian sniper, is one of the unit's primary functions. Another, of course, is to harass and deter Syrian commandos attempting to infiltrate across Israeli lines on intelligence-gathering or sabotage assignments during the dreaded snows of winter.

Special operations in the snow, especially when the powdery white stuff is found in the Middle East, is as much a game of intimidation as anything else. The mere existence of the Alpinistim is a deterrent; Israel's ability to despatch skiborne commandos to attack a Syrian position is enough to preempt any hostile move against an Israeli position. Intimidation is very important to the commandos of the unit as well. When skiing close to Syrian lines, they make a point of pulling a woolen ski mask over their face to add a devilish appearance to their swift and fluid movements on the snow.

Sergeant Major Benny, twenty-four, is a Sayeret Golani veteran and Alpinistim NCO and a person who has seen too much combat for one his age. Supervising the evacuation of a "wounded" comrade under fire, he was asked, "If war erupts, are you ready for the Syrians?" Standing silently amid the stoic snowdrifts, he smiles and says, "The question should be, Are they ready for us!"

Chapter 5

Sayeret Giva'ati: Samson's Foxes

It was a merciful day in the Jordan Valley—only 50 degrees Celsius in the shade! The depression that surrounds the Jordan River and is enclosed by the majestic desert hills that separate Israel and Jordan from one another is an impassive example of the awesome beauty of nature and the desolate power it possesses. The landscape in the valley is, indeed, barren. The sandy hills have been carved into unique shapes by the gusting winds and the course of thousands of years; they are both dizzying and confusing. The only interruptions to the sea of sand are the occasional Bedouin encampment, a palm tree or two, and, on this summer's morning, a thin, green line of soldiers marching at a feverish pace.

For the commandos of Sayeret Giva'ati, the reconnaissance company of the elite Giva'ati Infantry Brigade, the inferno of the Jordan Valley is but a geographic landmark that is negotiated during a forced march. This particular forced march is in the middle stage of its 120km course. Gold, albeit "purple gold," lies at the end of this rainbow, however. This is the Masa'a Kumtah, or Beret March. In a small, close-knit force such as Sayeret Giva'ati, unit pride is everything. For soldiers in the Giva'ati Infantry Brigade, pride means the purple beret—even if it takes an impossible 120km of bone-breaking marching to get it.

The long line of soldiers do not appear properly dressed for the task at hand. Each commando carries an Israeli soldier's usual burden of basic fatigues, load-bearing web gear filled to capacity with ammunition, grenades, medical equipment, canteens, a Kevlar ballistic helmet strapped to the chin, and a rucksack filled with other bits of *heavy* equipment. Naturally, since this is the IDF, each soldier carries a Pa'kal, or squad support item, at all times; this can be a jerry can with water filled to capacity, a stretcher, a field

The Giva'ati Brigade's desert rats, circa 1948. Three jeepborne desert commandos from Shu'alei Shimshon, the 54th Battalion's reconnaissance and shock force, race toward an engagement with Egyptian forces near Beersheba.

radio, an RPG, an LAW rocket, a mortar, or a rucksack filled with antitank rifle grenades. Under normal circumstances, such as the Spartan comfort of being inside an M113s APC, the Pa'kal is a minor annoyance. During a forced march, however, it is added weight and an additional strain to one's back and leg muscles that makes negotiating vast stretches of inhospitable territory an impossible task. The commandos, of course, are trained to surpass the impossible and to carry one additional

A stoic Sayeret Giva'ati officer gazes through his field glasses, too close for comfort to terrorist country in southern Lebanon. The Glilon SAR is always close at hand.

piece of equipment; in fact, the issued item has become an extension of their very body.

Beyond the regular gear, beyond the Pa'kal, and beyond the heat is the commando's personal weapon. A Glilon 5.56mm assault rifle weighs in at 4kg; a CAR-15 5.56mm assault weapon weighs over 3kg. Slung over every commando's shoulder on a tattered khaki canvas sling, the weapon's weight intensifies with each kilometer that has been logged. It is heavy after 5km, a tremendous burden after 30km. After 80km, it is a dagger stabbing through the shoulder of each soldier. When the Sayeret Giva'ati commander decides the time is right to pick up the pace and "run" a little, the weapon will begin to jump up and down and bang into muscles that desperately need a rest and against bones that have already taken too much abuse for a single day.

A lot of running will be done this sweltering morning, and already there are signs of trouble. The soldiers' uniforms are all drenched with perspiration and caked with dust, several fractures have been incurred, and nearly one dozen marchers are beginning to show signs of dehydration—when the company commander says, "Drink," you had better drink! Other soldiers, having slipped on the treacherous sands or slid down a rocky ravine, must bandage their bleeding knees in step in order not to be left out of the march's synchronized pace. In true IDF fashion, several stretchers have been opened, and a few of the Sayeret Giva'ati hopefuls who have turned an ankle or opted not to drink their required canteenful of water find themselves on their back being carried by comrades who, themselves, look as if they should be carried. The ambulance that follows the procession has yet to accept a customer this day, since nobody is willing to accept the defeat of falling to the body's own limitations.

The 120km must be negotiated in exactly 26 hours—that means 4.62km per hour. The grueling pace is, indeed, a tremendous burden placed on these young soldiers, but, after all, they should be used to it. Most have been members of Giva'ati Brigade for over a year. They have been subjected to countless challenges in their brief, though action-filled, military career, but no test put before them—not an operational foray along the Lebanese frontier nor a major wintertime exercise in the bitter cold atop the Golan Heights—is as treacherous as the Beret March.

The Giva'ati Brigade's purple beret, a striking and colorful emblem of unit pride, is as important to a soldier in Sayeret Giva'ati as the silver metal parachutist wings are to a commando from Sayeret Tzanhanim, and the flying tiger to a commando from Sayeret Golani. Most important, without succeeding in the Beret March, the trainee cannot defeat the ultimate challenge: passing Sayeret Giva'ati training! The Beret March is a rite of passage as crucial to a soldier's acceptance into the Giva'ati Brigade and its Sayeret as is the bar mitzvah or bat mitzvah celebration to a Jewish child turning into an adult. Once the soldiers in Sayeret Giva'ati training successfully complete the Beret March, they are tentatively welcomed into the Giva'ati Brigade's family of fighters. The challenge to remain in the unit, however, will last throughout their career.

The Giva'ati Brigade is one of the oldest of Israel's fighting units. A part of the Haganah's Field Corps of the late 1930s, Giva'ati was created as a conscript, regular force of trained soldiers to be mobilized at a moment's notice. When, in November 1947, the Haganah High Command created its six conventional brigades to repel the expected and inevitable Arab invasion, the 5th Giva'ati Infantry Brigade was responsible for defensive operations in the southern portion of Israel. Like all Israeli fighting formations of its time, the brigade was understaffed, was poorly equipped, and consisted of very few conventional arms and meager resources of ammunition.

When the 1948 War of Independence commenced a day following Israel's declaration of independence, the Giva'ati Brigade was propelled into immediate and bloody action. Gen. Ya'akov Dori, chief of staff of the IDF, had confidence in the brigade as a result of the decisive and brilliant leadership of its commander, Lt. Col. Shimon Avidan, and saw great potential with it, especially following its spectacular defensive actions against the massive Egyptian invasion in the south, and he decided to improve it one step further. At a time when most Israeli brigades were receiving new immigrants—mainly Holocaust survivors who the

British had interned on Cyprus—who could not speak Hebrew and had no military training whatsoever as front-line soldiers, the 5th Giva'ati Brigade was given a generous supply of former U.S. Army jeeps and lavish supplies of German MG34 light machine guns. Giva'ati's 54th Battalion, the brigade's best, was about to receive its own, indigenous, reconnaissance company. It would be known as Shu'alei Shimshon—Samson's Foxes.

For a unit thrown together in the midst of a desperate war for national survival, Shu'alei Shimshon performed remarkably. In the footsteps, or jeep tire marks, of Capt. David Stirling's Long Range Desert Group, Shu'alei Shimshon were truly Israel's "desert rats": roaming the wasteland of the Negev Desert in open jeeps with mounted machine guns, they harassed Egyptian troop formations with devastating surprise attacks. The unit particularly enjoyed striking in the low light of dawn. Charging toward its target in the mechanized version of a cavalry charge, the force of jeeps would race through the dunes and obliterate enemy encampments with its machine gun fire and volleys of tossed grenades. Shu'alei Shimshon's presence in the southern theater of operations,

An exhausted Sayeret Giva'ati hopeful is barely capable of maintaining his comrade in place on a stretcher during the unit's Gibush test period.

along with the operations of the Pal'mach's Negev Brigade, was a key in helping the fledgling IDF withstand Egypt's initial advance and push the mighty Arab armies back into the Sinai Peninsula.

The 1948 War was more than a turning point for the Giva'ati Brigade—it was the brigade's ultimate high point. Following the conflict, the unit saw limited service in the consolidated and frugal IDF of the 1950s. Reduced to a mechanized infantry force by 1960, it was slowly phased out of operational service and diminished to a source of great folklore.

The days of 1948 and 1956 are long gone. The new and revamped Giva'ati Infantry Brigade was restored to its historic spot in the IDF's order of battle in 1983. Lebanon had taught the IDF the importance of an amphibious-capable force of infantry soldiers, much like the U.S. Marines, that can race off of a landing vessel and storm an enemy beach. When, on the night of June 6–7, 1982, the IDF launched its largest ever amphibious assault on Sidon, on the first day of Operation Peace for Galilee, it was the paratroop brigade, equipped with M113s and reinforced by a force of Centurion tanks, that hit the beach in Iwo Jima style. The operation was a brilliant success, but the paratroopers encountered more difficulties en route to their landing than they did once on the shore opposite Palestinian terrorist units. Unaccustomed to the pitched rolls of a ship in motion on the open seas, many of the paratroopers suffered terrible spasms of seasickness and landed in horrible shape.

What the IDF needed was a force of marines, and since the U.S. Marine Corps, a living and breathing role model, was only a few hundred

While a Sayeret Giva'ati Gibush commander sits comfortably on the warm desert sands and takes a puff on his pipe, two Sayeret trainees carry themselves, *their gear, weaponry, and, of course, a very heavy sand-bag during a brief 20km march.*

meters away from Israeli lines garrisoning Beirut International Airport as part of the Multi-National Front, it was decided to emulate the originals. Instead of piecing a brigade together with separate elements from the Golani Brigade, the paratroopers, and the Armored Corps, the decision was made to start from relative scratch. The new unit was aptly named the Giva'ati Brigade in deference to an historic and successful force that had been on the shelf for over twenty years. Foreign sources reported that the new brigade was meant to operate in concert with the IDF's sizable fleet of Soviet-produced tanks, primarily T-54s, T-55s, and T-62s, that were captured from the Syrian and Egyptian armies during the past three wars and have since been reequipped with 105mm guns and new fire control systems, rearmored, and renamed Tiranim.

Naturally, when the Giva'ati Brigade was reborn into the IDF's order of battle, the new brigade was destined to have its own *indigenous* reconnaissance company. Initially, however, it is believed that the Giva'ati Brigade received a ready-made Sayeret—the remnants of what was once a premier reconnaissance formation, Sayeret Shaked. IDF Southern Command's reconnaissance force had for years been a mobile group of Bedouin trackers and paratroop-trained border patrol soldiers that protected southern Israel, along the precarious Egyptian and Jordanian frontiers, against infiltration attempts by Palestinian guerrillas, hashish and gun smugglers, and enemy

A newcomer to the State of Israel from Ethiopia and veteran Giva'ati Brigade trooper attempts to prove his worth as a member of Shu'alei Shimshon during a nighttime forced stretcher march.

espionage agents. Racing across the frontier on a few mechanically unstable jeeps fitted with a machine gun and a field radio, they mastered vast stretches of territory through sheer tenacity. For the most part, however, they patrolled the desert on foot. In the epic tradition of Beau Geste, the Long Range Desert Group, and the Giva'ati Brigade's own Samson's Foxes from the 54th Battalion, the soldiers of Sayeret Shaked became impeding fixtures of the desert—a jeep was their camel, and the desert belonged to them. Their commander was a legendary officer, and Bedouin Arab who had at one time fought the Jews, named Amos Yarkoni. Virtually every Israeli commando officer since the late 1950s has been influenced by Yar-

koni's courageous method of command under fire —he lost an eye and an arm in battle—and tactics for reconnoitering frontier areas.

By 1983, however, Sayeret Shaked was a far cry from its once glorious standing and became a mechanized battalion staffed by reconnaissance paratroopers. Since the Giva'ati Brigade of days past had once been responsible for defensive operations in Southern Command, the new brigade's home, too, would be in the south. The reconnaissance commandos from Sayeret Shaked would make the transformation into the framework of the new modern brigade and serve as an example to the rest of the fledgling force. Naturally, they would adopt the name of the Giva'ati Bri-

As Sayeret Giva'ati Gibush commanders watch silently, reconnaissance commando hopefuls undergo a grueling and physically challenging obstacle course, *carrying a person's weight in sand on a stretcher for added difficulty.*

gade's old Pal'Sar, or Reconnaissance Company: Shu'alei Shimshon.

Colonel Y., the Giva'ati Brigade commander, said: "What Samson's Foxes did in '48 is really nice for nostalgia but doesn't mean much today. What's important to me is what the Sayeret does now, and how we look in the field! There is a saying, Where the paratroopers can walk, Giva'ati has to run. When we screw up, nobody ever recalls the days of the unit in 1948. We have to prove ourselves on a day-to-day basis, hour to hour, more than any other brigade in the Army."

Because the modern-day Samson's Foxes is the newest reconnaissance or commando force in the Israeli military, it has the most to prove. This is a burden the unit feels is unfair but accepts. According to Sergeant Noam, a Sayeret Giva'ati NCO for two years: "We have a saying in the brigade that Giva'ati is hard like all other [brigades], but much fairer! Well, in the Sayeret, it is much harder than anywhere else, yet nobody is fair to us."

Unit pride is a tremendous motivator behind the success of a military formation; it is one element behind the issuance of a unique purple Giva'ati beret and easily identifiable Giva'ati Brigade unit tag. On a more personal level, the desire to have the combined efforts of soldiers who have trained incessantly to reach a stage of military preparedness and capability, and have their skills

Sayeret Giva'ati volunteers find themselves faced with impossible physical obstacles—such as carrying themselves and their stretcherful of sand over a wall barrier. Nobody said that serving in Shu'alei Shimshon would be easy, and only a special breed of fighter can wear the unit's reconnaissance wings.

Sayeret Giva'ati soldiers carry their Zodiac craft to the water before perfecting the art of conducting a coastal intelligence-gathering mission.

duly appreciated, can motivate a soldier to march farther, run faster, or lob a grenade with greater accuracy. Pushing the unit to be the best is Captain Y.'s job.

Along the shores of southern Israel, just due north of the Gaza Strip, the stage is set for a large-scale amphibious exercise. Several IDF Navy landing craft, mainly former U.S. ships frugally pulled out of mothballs, will hit the surf and unload a mini invasion force of infantry soldiers and M113s that are to cut a slice through "enemy" territory and link up with forces advancing up the coastal plain from a different axis. During wartime, the IAF would fly close-cover and protect the amphibious force from any obvious military threat, but the IAF cannot race through the beach to ensure that a well-camouflaged force of antitank commandos, armed with RPGs and Sagger missiles, is not lying in wait. It cannot ensure that the main road to be traveled is not littered with booby-trapped devices or that a series of deserted buildings overlooking

As a corporal instructor looks on, Sayeret Giva'ati trainees are offered the basics in a rowing exercise.

the roadways is not hiding vast numbers of enemy forces. That type of work belongs to the Sayeret.

An hour before the main Giva'ati force will land, a small team of naval commandos arrives on shore and checks to see if the beach has been booby-trapped with explosives and land mines. If the area has, indeed, been prepared by the enemy, then an alternative landing site will have to be found. All is clear this summer's dawn, however. The Flotilla 13 commandos signal in a lead IDF Navy landing craft holding two dozen Sayeret Giva'ati infantry soldiers and five jeeps. The moment the landing craft's ramp drops down into the surf, three of the jeeps are to race out and break out of the beach area and into the heart of "enemy" territory. The jeeps are heavily armed with machine guns, and a few with mounted TOW antitank guided weapons, and are meant to blaze a path toward the rendezvous point inland. They are not to stop and examine every suspicious item en route. They are simply to reconnoiter and report. That is their job, that is their mandate. Naturally, should they come under enemy fire, they are more than equipped, with firepower and combat skill, not only to defend themselves, but to attack, and dominate, as well.

Obviously, the tension of actually being in enemy territory does not loom over the heads of the Sayeret Giva'ati infantry soldiers racing across a dirt path along a ravine. Although the adrenaline of operations in Lebanon, something each of these Samson's Foxes has experienced countless times before, does not race through their system in this exercise in southern Israel, they feel definite pressure. They must cross a predetermined stretch of territory in a predesignated time slot. Any deviance from their meticulous and demanding schedule could ruin the offensive plans of an entire brigade. In wartime, thousands of lives could be on the line.

The exercise goes off well, and Captain Y. is pleased with the results. All the jeeps have stuck to their itinerary perfectly.

The training operation on the shores of the Mediterranean was assisted by another "elite" unit within the Giva'ati Infantry Brigade: Pal'Han—the acronym for Engineering Company—Giva'ati. The brigade's sapper force, Pal'Han Giva'ati has fought to prove itself in much the same way as has the brigade's Sayeret. Forced to compete with the Golani Infantry Brigade's own elite engineering and sapper force, the Giva'ati engineers have been pushed further and harder than perhaps any similar unit in the IDF; they have earned their elite reputation through blood and sweat.

In this exercise, Pal'Han Giva'ati is the second force to land and follows the Sayeret, blowing up potential ambush positions and clearing a path for the remainder of the brigade to cross. The Purple Beret explosive experts are appreciated by the rest of their brigade for their multiple talents: they are part foot soldier, part demolitions expert, and, because they are tasked with preparing ambushes deep in the heart of enemy territory, part reconnaissance commando, as well. Pal'Han Giva'ati has seen much action in southern Lebanon, where it has battled Palestinian terrorists attempting to reach the Israeli border as well as Shi'ite gunmen from Hizbollah eager to martyr themselves with a car bomb or in a suicide assault.

Sayeret Giva'ati, too, has seen much action in Lebanon. The Purple Beret reconnaissance com-

Having secured a beachhead for the remainder of the brigade, Sayeret Giva'ati commandos watch as Giva'ati mechanized elements land on the shores of southern Israel during amphibious operation exercises.

mandos have been quite active across the notorious Purple Line since the early 1980s.

Much to the chagrin of many Giva'ati Brigade commanders, the Purple Berets had been used primarily in a defensive role while stationed along the Lebanese frontier. All of the brigade's battalions and units have served a stint along the imposing fence separating Israel and Lebanon; they have patrolled the sandy dirt road along the fence, and they have lain in ambush inside Israel's self-imposed security zone, where they have battled terrorists in epic firefights and battles. They have fought the enemy well and have earned a high-profile reputation as a topnotch combat unit. Needless to say, this reputation has had a dear price. Many Giva'ati soldiers have fallen in battle, even more have been wounded; many of these casualties have been officers, including young lieutenants who, in the granite tradition of Israel's elite unit commanders, have led from the front and been killed while guiding their soldiers in battle.

Special operations in Lebanon, however, were never given to Sayeret Giva'ati: perhaps the IDF General Staff didn't have the proper faith invested in the unit; perhaps Northern Command did not appreciate the true capabilities of the Shu'alei Shimshon. In any event, when the call came in to conduct a covert long-range "special forces"–type mission across the security zone into the bandit country of southern Lebanon's Hizbollah-land, Sayeret Golani or Sayeret Tzanhanim got the call.

Everything changed on Thursday night, April 19, 1990. To deter Hizbollah from even thinking about attacking IDF or SLA positions inside the

A Sayeret Giva'ati platoon commander and his radio-man lie next to a target while awaiting the landing of the remainder of the brigade.

security zone, Sayeret Giva'ati was finally given a "special op." It was to hit the heart of Hizbollah's base of operations in the Maidun–E' inAtina–Masha'ara triangle of villages, mountains, and caves north of the security zone. The objective of the operation was to surprise the terrorists as they went about their daily business of preparing for suicide strikes against Israeli positions. The raid was, according to one Sayeret Giva'ati officer, supposed to "shake things up for the terrorists." It was to ruin their daily routine and take them seriously off balance, where they would be vulnerable to further Israeli attacks; it was also a search-and-destroy operation. Because of the difficult terrain and the enemy the Israelis were encountering, the success of the mission was dependent less on a helicopter transport or fast-moving jeeps than on the mighty legs of the Sayeret Giva'ati infantry soldiers, their lightning-fast trigger fingers, and their cohesion first as teams, then as platoons, and finally as a company.

Sayeret Giva'ati crossed the loosely fortified borders of the security zone just after midnight. The terrain that needed to be negotiated was hellish: steep hills, sudden drops into treacherous wadis, thorny bushes, and rolling boulders. The Sayeret Giva'ati task force was split into several smaller components, usually comprising a team or two, and in constant coordination with the brigade C^3 post situated a few klicks back and with Major A., the task force commander.

Throughout the night, the Sayeret Giva'ati commandos made their presence known to the local population. Suspicious movements of people confirmed not to be civilians were deterred by gunfire. Finally, after nearly 12 hours in enemy territory, one Sayeret Giva'ati team came upon a force of heavily armed Hizbollah gunmen heading toward Israeli lines. The Israelis spotted them first and launched a murderous, though brief, barrage of automatic fire at the terrorists. The Hizbollah fighters never had a chance. Two of them were killed before they realized that Israeli commandos were in their midst. Several other Hizbollah gunmen were wounded and managed to escape.

Upon examining the bodies of the two dead terrorists, the Sayeret Giva'ati commandos found several assault weapons and loads of explosives.

They were tempted to pursue the other Hizbollah fighters from the seven-person terrorist squad, but a high enemy body count was not the principal objective of this mission. The true purpose behind the foray was its psychological effect on the Hizbollah warlords. You have nowhere to hide from us, was the Israeli message, nowhere to run. We will hunt you down whenever we want, and we will invade your territory at will. Nevertheless, four additional Hizbollah terrorists were killed by another Sayeret Giva'ati team a few kilometers deeper into Lebanese territory. The Shi'ite guerrillas attempted to engage the Giva'ati troopers with small arms and LAW rocket fire, but before they could prepare the tube launchers for firing, they were cut down by the Sayeret Giva'ati team—proving that nothing is more lethal than a member of Shu'alei Shimshon with an FN MAG!

Upon their return to Israeli territory, after over 16 hours in Lebanese territory, the Giva'ati commandos and infantry soldiers were greeted by the commander of IDF Northern Command, Maj. Gen. Yossi Peled, a remarkable officer who, as a child in war-torn Belgium, had escaped death in the Holocaust. As the fighters in combat fatigues

Unimpressed by his unit's attempts to storm a beach, a Sayeret Giva'ati officer offers some choice words to a reconnaissance team and orders it to do it all again— until it does it right!

with tired faces returned through an opening in the border fence, a smiling Major General Peled gazed upon them and said: "I salute the Giva'ati Brigade that performed a *classic* infantry attack in the best possible light under the most difficult of topographical and defensive conditions, without enduring any casualties while achieving decisive results. The Giva'ati Brigade *now* joins the IDF's other 'chosen' units that have, in their history, conducted spectacular and successful operations behind enemy lines in Lebanon."

The Sayeret Giva'ati infantry soldiers appreciated the kind words from the OC Northern Command, but they were more receptive to the words of the operation's commander, Major A., who said:

"We did what we had been taught to do, and now, thanks to you, Giva'ati is on the map. I am sure that this operation will secure similar assignments in the future." The new Giva'ati Brigade commander, Col. Giora Inbar, himself a former Sayeret Golani and reconnaissance officer, was equally as proud of *his* new reconnaissance company. Back at the border, the burly officer who had seen many special forces–type operations in his own illustrious career, greeted each fighter personally; a pat on the back and a smile from the Mefaked Chativa (Ma'Chat), or Brigade Commander, was worth more than all the headlines in the world.

Sayeret Giva'ati did not have time to recover from its difficult, though highly successful, mis-

Well concealed behind a dune's foliage, a Sayeret Giva'ati officer and his communications support team *prepare to probe deeper into enemy territory during amphibious landing exercises.*

sion in southern Lebanon; the unit had an incessant schedule of training on its itinerary. From the bitter mountains of southern Lebanon where the picturesque hills were dotted with the dangers of Hizbollah to an anonymous training facility somewhere on the Golan Heights, Sayeret Giva'ati needs to work itself frantic in order to achieve the recognition it so deserves.

Back in the real world of Israel, at the base area of the Golan Heights, the commandos of Sayeret Giva'ati were again at work perfecting one of their true special talents: water crossing. Since the Giva'ati Brigade was intended to be the Israeli version of the U.S. Marines, amphibious and water operations became a Giva'ati, especially a Sayeret Giva'ati, exclusivity. Amphibious operations, such as landing on a hostile beach complete with armor support, are difficult maneuvers where multiser-

vice coordination is a prerequisite in achieving success and victory. Fording a river obstacle on a rubber raft, however, is a more personal type of operation. Crossing a river, with stealth, doesn't depend on the seafaring capabilities of a landing craft skipper or on tidal charts and shore defenses. It is the tenacity of heavily armed soldiers, loaded down with flak vests, web gear, and life preservers, who must row in a coordinated effort in order to secure victory. It is teamwork pure and simple. The coordination of a Sayeret team is a true personification of every IDF reconnaissance formation— especially Sayeret Giva'ati.

During the 1967–70 War of Attrition, Sayeret Golani mounted dozens of riverine commando strikes against Palestinian terrorist positions across the Jordan River. The domain of crossing the Jordan River or Lebanon's Litani or Awali rivers

Having performed their role as beach probers perfectly, elements from Sayeret Giva'ati return to their IDF

Navy landing vessel following the successful completion of their training exercise.

belongs to Sayeret Giva'ati. The objective of this training exercise is for a force from Sayeret Giva'ati to cross a river water obstacle and land its fighters on the opposite bank so that they can sabotage an enemy position. It is dawn, and the sun's first rays have emerged across the mountain peaks and are beginning to shine, ever so faintly, into the tree line. The streaks of light are Sayeret Giva'ati's invitation to the exercise. The fighters all wear their combat equipment underneath what is known in the IDF Navy as a German life vest. It is cumbersome and uncomfortable and makes quick and silent rowing, a must if the force is to reach its target without a splashing warning, a most difficult task. Six men ride in each boat, and the reconnaissance commandos lift the heavy rubber raft by its surrounding ropes and quickly run with

it into the water. A small splash is produced, but nothing too loud. The commandos assemble themselves into their rubberized ferries in a meticulous choreography of proper weight so that the craft will not tip over. In all, six boats are in the water this day; naturally, Second Lieutenant Amir, a Sayeret Giva'ati platoon commander and the senior officer participating in the exercise, is in the lead boat.

The boats are at their most vulnerable when in the middle of the river and can be blown out of the water by a determined enemy equipped with even the simplest of weapons, such as an automatic rifle. To provide something of an equalizing effect, or at least a point of cover fire, a Sayeret Giva'ati commando sits at the tip of the rubber boat clutching an FN MAG 7.62mm light machine

At an informal chin-wag with the OC Southern Command, the brigade commander, and other senior officers—along with their children!—Sayeret Giva'ati troopers are offered a chance to vent some steam or try an idea or two with the top brass. The IDF, especially its special forces, is an egalitarian army.

gun—one hand holding the cloth wrapped around the bipod, one hand surrounding the trigger housing, and the gunner's eagle eye peers through the sights, selecting potential targets. The river obstacle is not very grand this morning, but it takes the reconnaissance force nearly 15 minutes to reach the other side. The boats are brought to within 2m of the river's opposite bank, and the Sayeret Giva'ati soldiers leap into the water and hit the beaches in much the same way that Allied soldiers hit Normandy during D-day in the Second World War.

Second Lieutenant Amir, clutching his CAR-15 carbine, assembles his fighters with a series of hand motions, and the force, thirty-six strong, begins a quick, though paced, race into the woods ahead. After jogging briskly for nearly 20 minutes, Second Lieutenant Amir's commandos reach an opening turned into an impromptu firing range. Most IDF maneuvers of this type eventually conclude with a live-fire exercise; it is important to determine how the physical stress of reaching an objective, and the fatigue it produces, affects a soldier's ability to fire a weapon accurately.

At the firing range are several Giva'ati officers; some hold field glasses to see the results of the work on the range, others hold charts. Each reconnaissance infantry soldier enters the firing range individually, runs in through a mini obstacle course of tires strewn about the floor and is then ordered to fire an eight-round semiautomatic burst standing in the upright position. The beating

Smiling because he can drop his target with one shot, a Sayeret Giva'ati trooper peers through his sniper scope and clutches his modified CAR-15 during company maneuvers.

rhythm of eight 5.56mm rounds exiting the barrel of the soldier's Glilon is a pleasing sound to officers observing the display. The Sayeret Giva'ati soldier is then asked to do ten pushups and told to fire another eight rounds in a kneeling position. Finally, the exhausted trooper fires the remainder of the thirty-round clip in the comfortable prone position. The exercise is repeated thirty or so times, until everyone has had a chance to fire off a full magazine of ammunition.

Although the IDF's command structure has recently been concerned about a sharp decline in basic marksmanship, the scores this warm spring morning are good— very good!

Captain Y. explained that a principal reason the new Giva'ati Brigade's reconnaissance force adopted the name Shu'alei Shimshon was that it adopted the old force's principal means of deployment: a jeep complete with an FN MAG 7.62mm fitted to the passenger's side for lightning assaults. The new unit's modus operandi was too similar to the old unit's for the name not to be the same; marching, however, would remain a unit talent. Most Sayeret Giva'ati fighters, however, would pay their life's earnings even just to see a jeep. Sayeret Giva'ati means marching. If it took 120km to earn a purple beret in the Sayeret, then to prove a fighter's capabilities for the top brass means 130km!

A force of Sayeret Giva'ati kneels behind a Centurion MBT that slowly advances along a desert path. Joint maneuvers between the Giva'ati Brigade's Sayeret and the rest of the IDF are crucial in coordinating cohesive offensive strategies during war.

Somewhere in the eastern Negev Desert, in a spot between two hills that look like the two hills passed over 30km earlier, it is day three of a seven-day period where the fighters of Sayeret Giva'ati can prove their worth as reconnaissance commandos; it is a test that every Giva'ati recon fighter must endure and persevere through. It is Hell Week.

This grueling period is one of the IDF's unique means for proving to itself that a soldier adorned

A force of Sayeret Giva'ati commandos is offered the opportunity to let off some steam—a task, as indicated by the sea of spent 7.62mm cartridges, that it accomplishes with zeal.

Sayeret Giva'ati comrades-in-arms display the Giva'ati Brigade's powerful purple colors.

During Hell Week, somewhere around kilometer number 100, one Sayeret Giva'ati trooper assists a comrade-in-arms as they attempt to negotiate a tricky climb of sliding sand and rocks.

with the reconnaissance identification is worthy of belonging to a Sayeret. Candidates leave home base equipped for some desperate hours. Beyond the web gear, flak vest, nuclear-biological-chemical (NBC) warfare equipment, helmet, protective goggles, and, of course, weapon, each Sayeret Giva'ati commando carries a rucksack filled to capacity with over 50kg of food, water, medical gear, and other necessities of survival in the field—from a shovel to a sleeping bag. Each fighter chooses what to take and is "advised" to take the absolute minimum that will supplement the daily nutritional requirements. Tasty staples such as packaged goods and junk food are replaced by meager supplies of dried fruits and grape sugar.

The commandos of Shu'alei Shimshon are to negotiate their 130km course without the benefit of maps, and without the benefit of help, usually by themselves—but always under the constant scrutiny of senior officers. The fighters follow their own itinerary in going from kilometer 1 to the magic number 130, but they must undergo a series of combat maneuvers in the middle of the long and arduous march.

Two Sayeret Giva'ati officers—First Lieutenant Guy, the deputy company commander, and First Lieutenant Ami, a team commander—are waiting at the bottom of a hill by their jeep when they notice a soldier, beleaguered and exhausted, gearing his body and the enormous load it carries for the sharp and quick trip downhill. As the soldier, eager to impress, gets closer to the two officers, they snicker and yell: "Gas attack. . . . Gas attack!" The poor recon commando produces a gas mask from one of his pouches and attempts to put it over his face in one fluid motion, but he is breathing too hard, and the puddle of sweat that covers his head causes the black mask to slide off in embarrassing fashion.

After a few seconds of juggling, the soldier is ready to negotiate a chemical environment. He is guided to an obstacle course peppered with nearly two dozen cardboard targets. Both Ami and Guy explain that he is to "engage" each target in a light run. The soldier flings his CAR-15 from around his shoulder, cocks the weapon, and prepares for action. The first two targets are engaged from a range of about 30m, but the soldier fires at what the two Sayeret Giva'ati officers looking on consider to be a relaxed pace. The soldier's gunfire is interrupted by menacing screams from supervising officers: "You are under fire, soldier.... They are firing at you.... Hurry!" He begins to attend to his task with greater seriousness, firing in quick, though deliberate, bursts as he runs through the maze. All of his shots hit their mark bunched very close together. Just what all commanders like to see of the fighters they will be leading into combat, where the firing will be for real.

The soldier completes his task well and soon joins another few members of his team. This time they must rappel down a 24m-high cliff and then attempt another obstacle course complete with cardboard targets. Already, most of the Sayeret Giva'ati soldiers undergoing Hell Week are no longer wearing a uniform considered acceptable

by the IDF: the olive fatigues are tattered and torn, and the green color has been removed by sweat. Anyway, whatever piece of uniform has remained intact will be ripped to shreds in the rappelling exercise. When the teams assemble below, several other Sayeret Giva'ati officers begin yelling, "al-Yahud," Arabic for "The Jews," and throwing rocks at the soldiers. It is time to move to a new firing range. Here, the soldiers are allowed to discharge two magazine loads of ammunition and are tested in throwing a grenade inside the center of a target. The unit also undergoes other combat exercises, but most are considered top-secret by the IDF.

The Sayeret Giva'ati commanders are concerned not that some of their charges will fail to complete the course, but rather about what level of professionalism those charges will actually perform at. Hell Week's supervising officers exam-

On May 30, 1990, reconnaissance infantry soldiers from Sayeret Giva'ati walk past a terrorist fast-attack craft and two discarded SA-7 missiles off the Israeli coast at Nitzanim, south of Tel Aviv, following their successful repulsion of a seaborne Palestinian terrorist attack by the Abu Abbas faction of the PLF.

ine and scrutinize every aspect of the seven-day period—from how long it takes a soldier to remove a grenade from its pouch, pull the pin, and toss it to its target, to how the soldier rolls on the ground into firing position. The candidates are also judged on more intuitive aspects of their art of soldiering. If they choose to sleep in a semicomfortable spot at the base of a hill or under a tree, they receive poor marks for exposing themselves to detection; if the soldiers choose to sleep inside a cave or dig a spot for themselves at the base of a boulder and cover themselves with leaves or branches, or even other rocks, they receive a high grade.

The entire purpose of Hell Week is to determine how the soldiers will fare in the field, deep behind enemy lines. Sayeret Giva'ati had proved itself more than capable of handling itself under such conditions. Should Israel have opted to participate in Operation Desert Storm and strike against Saddam Hussein, Sayeret Giva'ati would certainly have been in the vanguard of any Israeli action.

When the first Iraqi SCUD missiles were falling on Tel Aviv and Haifa in 1991, Sayeret Giva'ati was seeking out new talent in one of its

A Sayeret Giva'ati trooper emerges from a riverbank to assault an "enemy" target.

Gibush tests. By then, Giva'ati was no longer an obscure unit in the IDF's order of battle—it was a presence. The brigade's Sayeret was attracting an enormous amount of attention, a great deal of fanfare, and more volunteers than it could possibly accept.

The type of new soldier and seasoned NCO volunteering to serve in Samson's Foxes reflects the new Israel. In this Gibush, nervously carried out near a pile of gas mask pouches—just in case—several of the volunteers are new immigrants from the Soviet Union, individuals whose Hebrew bears a heavy Russian accent and whose desire to serve their new homeland is overwhelming. Quite a few Sayeret hopefuls in this Gibush are new immigrants to the Jewish State from Ethiopia: some of them came nearly ten years earlier during the Operation Moses airlift; some have been in Israel for only a couple of years, rescued from civil war in their native land during the Operation Solomon airlift.

Lieutenant Avi, one of the officers supervising the Gibush, likes the new immigrants. "They feel that because of their new status, language difficulties, and overall feeling of sticking out in a new country and culture, that they need to excel, they need to prove their worth by being the best. As a result, they push themselves and push the rest of the native-born Sabras [native Israelis] to be *that* much better." They will need to be. In the incessant competition to be the best of all IDF conventional reconnaissance formations, Sayeret Giva'ati has made enormous gains in the eyes of the General Staff. The unit has won the IDF competition for physical fitness as well as combat ability. To make sure that the Sayeret maintains its elite, overachieving reputation, the unit tolerates nothing less than perfection. The slightest screw-up can result in a recruit's ejection from Sayeret Giva'ati training. Each candidate is told this as fact, but they want to volunteer nonetheless. The right to serve in such an elite unit, to wear the coveted purple beret, and to have the Shu'alei Shimshon reconnaissance wings placed upon their chest is too much of a prize to relinquish without a fight. The Gibush continues.

At the same time as Sayeret Giva'ati hopefuls were trying to prove their worth at a facility somewhere in central Israel, a force of Sayeret Giva'ati commandos who had already passed the grueling selection and training process was busy racing throughout the Negev Desert abyss in a dozen jeeps, all heavily armed, and preparing to assault a fortified enemy position in a nearby sand dune. The reconnaissance soldiers were all equipped for prolonged action, loaded down with over 36kg of equipment, and armed with a wide variety of weaponry, from M-16s fitted with exotic sniper sights to Ma'Pa'Tz antitank missiles—the Israeli-produced version of the American TOW— carried by three-person crews. Also carried by each commando was a purple beret and an infantry beret badge made of brass—the sign and source of the unit's immense pride. Wherever it

was going and whatever it was doing, Sayeret Giva'ati was determined to leave its mark for all to see.

Sayeret Giva'ati was honing up on its skills in preparation for the intended raid against western Iraq. Samson's Foxes was ready to engage the Iraqi army; it was ready to roam the desert of western Iraq and decimate the SCUD missile launchers that had brought destruction and fear to the citizens of Israel. Sayeret Giva'ati never did get that trip to Iraq, but having the General Staff make it an integral element of the planned operation far from Israeli territory proved that the unit had, indeed, made its mark. Over forty years since it first made a name for itself, Sayeret Giva'ati, Samson's Foxes, was truly on the map!

At Nitzanim, a Sayeret Giva'ati officer looks at the PLF fast-attack craft that attempted to land a force of terrorists on the shores of Tel Aviv, while his radioman *maintains a hold on the remainder of the reconnaissance company for the possibility of further action.*

Chapter 6

Sayerot Ha'Druzim and Ha'Beduim

In northern Israel on May 1970, Haim Bar-Lev, IDF chief of staff, stands together with a group of Druze officers as they observe the newly created Sayeret Ha'Druzim conduct assault maneuvers on the Golan Heights.

It was dark in northern Israel; the only light was an eerie orange glow coming from a moon covered by imposing rain clouds. Suddenly, however, a flare shot up into the sky; its lurch was a muted whine that ended when the phosphorous light grenade erupted in midair and slowly came down to earth.

The flare was the signal for the attack to commence. A force of ten heavily armed soldiers, equipped with assault rifles and RPGs, began its approach to the target. All the commandos wore protective clothing to shield them from the harsh winter's cold and had a white and black Kefiyeh headdress wrapped around their necks and worn as a scarf. The force commander, clutching his AKMS assault rifle, held up one hand and signaled for the force to split into three groups. He would approach the target, a row of one- and two-story buildings, alone. Once he tossed in a grenade through the front door of the first building, the rest of the fighters, who had already sneaked past fortifications and positioned themselves around the other two buildings, would commence their attack.

The group leader, Salim, gingerly slunk his way across the perimeter illuminated by the flickering sparkle of the descending flare, pressed his back against the first building's wall, and produced a hand grenade from his ammunition pouch. Pulling the pin sharply, he tossed the fragmentation grenade through the main door and crouched to one knee as he allowed the 4 seconds to pass and the device to detonate in a thunderous blast. The explosion did not disappoint. Before the smoke cleared, Salim yelled, "Ya'Allah," a loose Arabic slang for "C'mon", and raked the room with a magazine-emptying burst of automatic fire. The two remaining squads followed suit. Within seconds, the entire objective was secured, and the force's radioman called in the remainder of the unit using a terse, cryptic Arabic code. Before Salim had the opportunity to discuss the raid with his commandos, they were joined by two dozen soldiers, their faces blackened with camouflaging grease. The night of fireworks had only just begun. The sounds of explosions would be heard throughout northern Israel until dawn.

These Arabic-speaking individuals were not armed intruders attacking an Israeli settlement or military installations, nor were they Palestinian terrorists or Syrian commandos. They were *Israeli* commandos. Druze Muslims, citizens of the Jewish State, conscripted into the ranks of the IDF and serving in a unique and remarkable reconnaissance formation: Sayeret Ha'Druzim, or Druze Recon, from Unit 300, an infantry force comprising members of minority groups.

A few dozen kilometers away from this training field in Israel's north, along the Jordanian-Israeli frontier near the Beit Shean Valley, two heavily armed Arabic-speaking men are milling about Israel's side of the fence. These men are Bedouins. They are trackers by trade, whose eagle eye instincts can, by following footprints and other physical marks left in the bush, detect the exact movements of a person—or beast—who has covered a particular stretch of open territory, be it a mountainous portion of the Negev Desert or a

Pleased with their prowess on the battlefield—and pleased with his decision to authorize their formation—Chief of Staff Bar-Lev addresses the commandos of Sayeret Ha'Druzim.

Sayeret Ha'Druzim soldiers pass through the terrain of northern Israel en route to assaulting a mock target. The sniper is equipped with an M-21; Sayeret Ha'Druzim snipers are among the best in the IDF.

mud-soaked plain in Galilee. For the Bedouins—tribal nomads of the deserts and hills—these traits are invaluable when trailing a lost sheep in the desert abyss; they are also quite useful when hunting down terrorists. The traits are inherent, taught to the young at an early age, and, like valuable heirlooms, are passed down from generation to generation.

The art of tracking is considered virtually exclusive to Bedouins. The Israelis realize this unique gift and have deployed their Bedouin soldiers, among the finest throughout the IDF, as trackers and scouts protecting border areas from infiltration attempts. Should a Palestinian terrorist, Islamic holy warrior, or Syrian or Jordanian commando attempt to cross one of Israel's four embattled frontiers, it will be the trackers' task to follow the intruder's movements and hunt him or her down; and the Bedouins usually are the first Israeli soldiers, meters ahead of a patrol and its commanding officer, to engage terrorists head-on.

These two trackers, A'bdallah and Falah, both wearing their tribal red-and-white-checkered Kef-iyeh headdress wrapped snugly around their heads, are patrolling a once-quiet frontier turned "hot" in recent years. Pro-Iraqi Palestinian terrorists, as well as deserting Jordanian soldiers who are members of the Islamic Jihad terrorist organization, have made numerous attempts to cross the border and perpetrate massacres against the nearby Israeli agricultural settlements.

It is the last minutes of an 8-hour patrol, yet both A'bdallah and Falah, serving with the elite Sayeret Ha'Na'Ha'L, (Na'Ha'L Recon), or Fighting Pioneer Youth Brigade's Reconnaissance Company, realize that this is *the* time when a terrorist would try to cross the frontier. The sun has just begun to rise over the striking purple sand hills to the east and will burn straight into the eyes of anyone gazing into Jordanian territory. Both trackers walk about 10m ahead of a heavily armed command car ferrying six Sayeret Ha'Na'Ha'L reconnaissance infantry soldiers along the fence and gear themselves for action. They walk slower than usual and have removed the safety from their M-16. The reconnaissance soldiers, too, gear for action. Sitting back to back, they are stationed at mounted RN MAGs aimed menacingly across the fence. The hissing squawking of radio chatter engulfs the desolate border area, but that annoying sound is virtually silenced by the rhythmic pounding of the trackers' heartbeats. Thankfully, nothing happens on *this* mission, but not all patrols end peacefully.

On the night of February 23, 1991, when the threat of a full-scale war between Israel and Iraq still existed, M. Sgt. Muhammed Shibli, thirty-four years old, was patrolling a stretch of the Jordanian border in the Jordan Valley, 10km north of Moshav Argaman, with a force of soldiers. Around midnight, he discovered the telltale signs of an infiltration: a small hole cut through the thick rows of concertina wire and footprints left in the dusty sand road. Flickering his flashlight to follow the prints, Master Sergeant Shibli raced into the desert hills, nearly 50m ahead of his accompanying troopers. Shibli knew what he was looking for and, through his desert instincts, knew where to look. After a brutal 1-hour pursuit through inhospitable terrain, he cornered the infiltrator in a gully and engaged the terrorist with his CAR-15. Master Sergeant Shibli was a good shot, and the terrorist, who was carrying an AK-47 and whose body was booby-trapped with explosives, was hit. He wasn't killed, however. The badly bleeding Palestinian gunman managed to unload several rounds in Master Sergeant Shibli's direction, and one round struck the Bedouin tracker, killing him instantly. The accompanying force of troopers finished the terrorist off seconds later with an unforgiving burst of machine gun fire.

Master Sergeant Shibli was buried the following day in his Galilee village of Shibli. Hundreds of comrades-in-arms and northern settlers paid their respects; among the mourners were Druze Muslims, Bedouins, and Circassians (members of a Muslim minority originating in Russia)—many of whom were trackers or veterans of the security forces—who stood in painful silence as one of their own was laid to rest. Master Sergeant Shibli was considered an effective and courageous tracker. He was always the first into battle, always displayed zeal and bravery in every engagement, and would pursue a suspected terrorist infiltration from sunrise to sunset—he would not rest until the terrorist had been hounded down. Master

Sergeant Shibli, a charismatic NCO who had excelled in paratrooper's basic training and jump school, was scheduled to begin officer's training later in the spring, and many believe he was being groomed to assume command one day of the newly created Bedouin reconnaissance commando force Sayeret Ha'Bedium, or Bedouin Recon. Lieutenant Colonel G., the IDF's chief tracker officer, said that Master Sergeant Shibli had a definite career in the Army, and no one could tell how far he would have gone.

Master Sergeant Shibli's dreams would go unfulfilled. He left behind a widow and five chil-

Having performed a series of grueling and impressive combat exercises, a young Sayeret Ha'Druzim smiles as he receives a few kind words from IDF top brass brought in for the show.

dren. A Bedouin and a Muslim had paid the ultimate price for protecting *his* country.

The existence of "Arab" soldiers in the ranks of the IDF is something of an anomaly in the Jewish State, and yet an inherent reality of the tumultuous and tribal world of the Middle East. Israelis are naturally suspicious of, and security sensitive to, anyone not Jewish; they are also pragmatic and realize that any help their outnumbered, outgunned, and beleaguered defense forces can obtain must be graciously accepted. Israelis, and the IDF in particular, also appreciate and adhere to the plurality of the Jewish State and the obligation of *all* of its citizens—Jews, Muslims, and Christians alike—to share the burden of its national defense. As a result, the minority soldiers saluting the Star of David at each morning inspection are much more than a racial mix of mercenaries risking life and limb for a mere salary of shekels. They are citizens of the State of Israel, separate but equal to the Jews, who realize that their unique cultures, religious sects, and tribal histories have fared far better under Jewish auspices than under the oppressive wrath traditionally endured in Lebanon, Syria, and Jordan.

Among the members of the minority, or Arab ethnic, groups serving in the IDF, the Druze Muslims are the most dominant and one of the two sects that are conscripted. The Druze are a mysterious offshoot of both the Sunni and Shi'ite versions of Islam, relying on an oral account of their faith rather than the scriptures of the Koran. They are descendants of the Ismailis, founders of the Fatimid Caliphate in the tenth century, who settled in the mountainous Lebanon-Syria-Palestine triangle. Although their language is Arabic, and their social and cultural patterns are almost identical to those of rural Muslim villagers, the Druze have often suffered from tense and hostile relations with the Muslim majorities who fear their secretive society. To overcome persecution, the Druze have become fierce nationalists. Druze in Lebanon's Shouf Mountains might be connected by faith and family to Druze living in Syria and Israel, but when it comes to defense of the homeland, they will fight and die with fanatic fervor—even if it means firing off shots in anger against their relatives in either Syria or Lebanon.

The Druze first volunteered into the IDF during the 1948 War, when all the non-Jewish (Arab) volunteers were shuffled into a mysterious melting pot of an infantry formation known as Unit 300; it was viewed as a minor, even somewhat amusing, side show. But the Druze, Circassians, and Bedouins who volunteered into Unit 300 cherished their military opportunity and struggled to prove their worth. The unit adopted a unique and martial motif of crossed Arabian scimitars over a Star of David, which they hoped would elevate them beyond second-class warrior status. In the field, they proved to be top-rate soldiers. Their specialty was combat in the wide-open spaces of the Negev Desert, where they saw action against Palestinian infiltrators and Arab intelligence agents crossing the borders from Egypt and Jordan. When Palestinian Fedayeen, or commando, attacks against Israeli frontier settlements began in the mid-1950s, the burden of border defenses fell primarily on minority units, whose inherent skills of the desert proved invaluable in

A senior Druze officer leads a group of Sayeret Ha'Druzim commandos on a patrol against Palestinian terrorists at the Lebanese border. Sayeret Ha'Druzim's counterterrorist operations along the Purple Line have become epic among commanders in Northern Command.

tracking down the cross-border raiders. The Druze were so successful and warmly accepted into the IDF, in fact, that in 1955, Druze elders approached Prime Minister David Ben-Gurion and demanded that their sons be conscripted into the IDF "like the Jews." So impressed was Ben-Gurion with the contribution of the Druze minority that he proudly proclaimed: "The pact between the Druze people and the Jewish people is not written on a scrap of paper. It is sanctified by the blood of the heroic Druze fighters."

Many Druze conscripts would volunteer for service in the National Police Border Guards. A small, though highly effective, force of professional frontier police, the Border Guards patrolled the most sensitive and volatile border outposts in jeeps and with small arms in hand. The Druze helped establish an elite esprit de corps in the Border Guards, eventually transforming service in its ranks into a family experience. It was, and remains, common for fathers, sons, and brothers all to serve in the Border Guards simultaneously. According to Druze tradition, when one family member falls in battle, another soon fills his place—taking possession of his bed, equipment, and place in formation.

During the 1967 Six Day War, the Druze-dominated Unit 300 took part in the fighting on the West Bank against the elite of King Hussein's Royal Jordanian army. When Druze soldiers captured the large West Bank town of Jenin, the local inhabitants—upon hearing their conquerors speak Arabic with a native flair—thought they had been liberated by the vanguard of an Iraqi expeditionary force rumored to be in the area. The Druze soldiers soon found themselves in the center of cheers, hugs, and barrages of wild orchids. The jubilant celebration ceased only when it was discovered that the soldiers' Uzi submachine guns were made in Israel, and the aerial antennas of the unit's vehicles were decorated with flags sporting the Star of David.

Following the war, the State of Israel realized that further conflict was inevitable; battle plans to face once again the Egyptian and Syrian armies were developed in IDF headquarters. One secretive, and yet fascinating, contingency plan was the formation of an elite Druze reconnaissance unit

known as Sayeret Ha'Druzim, or Druze Recon. The unit was the novel brain child of a firebrand Druze officer named Mohammed Mullah, a visionary way ahead of his time who was able to foresee the strategic demands of Israel's new frontiers and how Unit 300 fit into this new post-1967 picture. At first, however, Major Mullah envisioned dismantling the indigenous Druze unit and sending its fighters, who had proved their loyalty and capabilities during the 1967 War, to the paratroopers

A Sayeret Ha'Druzim NCO, his face embittered by the rough-and-tumble of service in Lebanon, gazes across the no man's land of the Beka'a Valley into lines occupied by Syrian commandos. The modified Glilon SAR and K-Bar commando knife are carried just in case the enemy gets a bit too close for comfort. Israeli Government Press Office

and Golani Infantry Brigade for "real" service. Yet, if the *regular* IDF was unwilling to integrate its ranks with the Druze, Circassian, and Bedouin fighters, then perhaps it was willing to allow Unit 300 to form its own elite subunit capable of special operations.

Unlike other armies, the IDF does not make proposing a novel idea a tremendous struggle against the obstacles of bureaucracy—it *loves* innovation. Major Mullah took his idea to Maj. Gen. David ("Dado") Elazar, then OC Northern Command and later chief of staff, who was so impressed with the notion that he immediately sent Mullah to Lt. Gen. Haim Bar-Lev, chief of staff. At the presentation, a nervous Mullah told Bar-Lev, "If we would form, for example, a parachutist-qualified Druze unit, a Sayeret of sorts, it could jump behind Syrian lines, in the Druze Mountains, should war erupt with Syria." Bar-Lev was enamored with the idea, and, because it belonged to Mullah and since Mullah was the highest-ranking Druze officer in the IDF, Mullah would be the new unit's commander. Sayeret Ha'Druzim was born.

Sayeret Ha'Druzim became a parachutist-qualified commando force of volunteers trained to infiltrate deep behind Syrian lines. Its members were capable of seizing the Druze villages along the road to Damascus and securing the approaches to the Syrian capital for advancing Israeli armor formations. When the 1973 War broke out, however, it was the Syrians—not the Israelis—who dictated the type of war that was to be fought. During the battle for the Golan Heights, Unit 300, by then elevated to the status of a brigade, fought with honor and distinction in brutal conflicts. Sayeret Ha'Druzim took part in the most emotional, and militarily important, operation of the campaign: the recapture of Mt. Hermon—the ultrasecretive intelligence-gathering post captured by Syrian commandos in the first hours of hostilities. During the two-day, close-quarter battle for Mt. Hermon, Sayeret Ha'Druzim played an essential role in its eventual recapture, proving its worth as a unit of eagle eye marksmen and displaying impressive physical prowess in the countless private hand-to-hand battles fought between themselves and the defending Syrian commandos.

When the IDF invaded Lebanon on June 6, 1982, Unit 300, with Sayeret Ha'Druzim in the forefront, found itself in much of the bitter fighting around the Palestinian refugee camps in southern Lebanon. But as the IDF pushed to Beirut, Israel's Druze fighters faced the deep dilemma of divided loyalty. The Israeli Druze once again faced their relatives serving in the Syrian army on the battlefield and were now placed in the awkward position of possibly engaging their fiercely independent Lebanese relatives devoted to warlord Walid Jumblatt's militia. Although the IDF did not engage the Lebanese Druze in "open" conflict, Israel was fervently supporting the historic nemesis of the Druze: the Maronite Christian Phalangists. In the madness of Lebanon, Christian and Druze had exchanged dozens of massacres, and it disturbed many of Israel's Druze soldiers that their nation, guided by Talmudic morals and a persecuted past, could openly support the "murderous" Phalangists.

A senior Druze officer addresses members of Sayeret Ha'Druzim and other Northern Command units during exercises atop the Golan Heights. To help the unit feel more accepted, Sayeret Ha'Druzim personnel are often taken to other reconnaissance and commando units to exchange ideas and experiences with other special forces soldiers.

Unit 300's combat record in Lebanon was impressive. With Sayeret Ha'Druzim leading most patrols and offensive actions against Palestinian positions, the Druze fought some of the most bitter battles of the war. The Druze, although constituting only 2 percent of the entire Israeli population, accounted for a significant percentage of Israel's war dead and wounded in Lebanon.

The heavy losses suffered by Druze fighters in Lebanon were a severe blow to the close-knit community. The sight of Druze elders presiding over the funerals of their fallen sons, with caskets draped in the Star of David flag, helped forge an undeniable bond between Jew and Druze. Today, Druze soldiers have broken out of the "minority ghetto" of Unit 300 to become paratroop, infantry, and armor officers, with one commander even reaching the rank of brigadier general.

A particularly interesting test of Sayeret Ha'Druzim's skills, both soldiering and diplomatic, occurred during the Intifadah. The unit was thrown into the uprising at a time when the "Jewish" soldiers, including those from various other Sayerot, were posting little success. Unit 300, Sayeret Ha'Druzim, and the Border Guards were called in as a last resort, and they surprised everyone but their own immediate commanders. Able to speak the language of the locals and intimate with the customs and sensitivities of the West Bankers and Gazans, the Druze recon soldiers combined cultural courtesy with an iron fist.

One Sayeret Ha'Druzim talent, a combat specialty that puts the unit a cut above every other "regular" Israeli reconnaissance formation, is its ability to maneuver in open country. In the mountainous brown fields of northern Israel, in the

A Sayeret Ha'Druzim FN MAG gunner team gazes across the deceivingly peaceful hills of southern Lebanon, in search of terrorist activity. Its obvious *linguistic skills make the unit a natural for operations in Lebanon.*

rolling hills turned green by harsh winter rains and an occasional snowstorm, the only interruption to the scenery is an occasional boulder. That is, of course, unless the field is under the control of Sayeret Ha'Druzim.

At a training position somewhere in Galilee, a force of recon infantry from Sayeret Ha'Druzim is slinking across a plush wadi toward a narrow roadway and a concrete building, three pillboxes, and rows of empty fuel drums up the opposite hill. The troopers do not wear camouflaged uniforms but are invisible to outside view. Using the method of crawling on the stomach and then getting quickly up to sprint 10 or 20m, the commandos are able to travel several kilometers and advance to within firing range of the road.

Crawling along the earth is a painful means of movement; small rocks and thorns that feel as if they can pierce even a Kevlar flak vest have ripped the flesh of many of the soldiers, and several are bleeding from their countless abrasions. These *minor* pains are not taken too seriously—they are par for the course. Ninety-five percent of the commandos in Sayeret Ha'Druzim are volunteers,

and they want to have rocks and thorns rip through their skin. It is how they prove their worth as fighters in the IDF.

Major M., the company commander, has already positioned himself 20m ahead of his unit, behind a boulder, and is gazing on the roadway through high-powered field glasses. The coast is clear. With his left hand raised, Major M. waves one time and gestures for one squad, including a MAG gunner and a grenadier with a LAW rocket, into firing position; the second hand gesture informs the sniper, Walid, to ready himself and his M-21 for action; finally, the third hand motion calls in the squad's grenadiers, two soldiers carrying RPGs and antitank rifle grenades. At H-hour, Major M. exposes himself from behind the boulder, crosses the road, and races up a steep incline toward the building. A segment of the force joins him in a well-choreographed assault, while the squads motioned in for support blanket the area with a devastating barrage of covering fire. The fuel drums kick up into the air as they are hit with rifle grenades, and the pillboxes crumble, succumbing to the armor-penetrating capabilities of RPG and LAW rockets. Moments later, the entire complex is overwhelmed by the Druze commandos. Several high-ranking officers looked on at the exercise, including the OC Northern Command. They were impressed with the display but not surprised. Sayeret Ha'Druzim has earned a tremendous reputation for itself in the last ten years.

Although this is an exercise, Sayeret Ha'Druzim has been extremely busy in recent years safeguarding the Purple Line on the Lebanese border, and engaging Palestinian terrorists attempting to cross into Israel. In this treacherous campaign, there is always the risk that the unit might find itself in combat against Lebanese Druze militiamen. It is not a daunting concern, however. According to Major M., "Our religion requires us to be loyal to the land and nation on which we live. We will do whatever is necessary in completing our mission and safeguarding our homes no matter who the enemy is." More often than not, the target at the other end of a Sayeret Ha'Druzim's gunsight will be a Palestinian terrorist or Hizbollah holy warrior attempting to reach the "fence."

Maj. Gen. Maton Vilnai, OC Southern Command, himself a former Sayeret Tzanhanim commander, pins the rank of second lieutenant to a newly commissioned Sayeret Ha'Druzim officer.

Like most of Unit 300's companies, Sayeret Ha'Druzim enjoys a truly unique *esprit de corps*, and one of the IDF's most impressive ceremonies in which the unit's spirit is implanted into the soldiers' souls is when new members of the Sayeret receive their wings. During the ceremony, a new force of Druze reconnaissance infantrymen, their faces beaming with pride and their parents and families and religious elders looking on, will have the small winged symbol of their distinction pounded into their chest by the unit's master sergeant. Following the emotional ceremony, a lamb will be slaughtered and the unit will celebrate in a fashion like only Sayeret Ha'Druzim can—a tremendous and traditional feast! After the festivities, the IDF will show its respect to the new unit. Representatives from the other Sayerot will address the new recon soldiers and formally accept them into Israel's commando family.

Although the Druze are the best known of Israel's minority soldiers serving in the IDF, the nomadic Bedouin tribes are, perhaps, the most romantic. In the close-quarter battle for the northern Galilee town of Safed during the frantic days of the 1948 War, the beleaguered and overwhelmed Jewish forces fighting Syrian army regulars were shocked to see a cavalry charge of Bedouin elders on white Arabian stallions racing to their aid. The charge of the Arab-al-Hayeb tribe was the first joint military venture between Bedouin and Jew and the forging of a much-cherished friendship. Bedouins, impressed by the Jews' acceptance of their nomadic traditions, volunteered into the IDF

A Bedouin tracker, nervously clutching his Glilon SAR, examines potentially dangerous prints in the mud opposite the Jordanian frontier.

A Druze tracker, serving in an elite Border Guard company garrisoning the northern frontier with Lebanon, takes a brief, though traditional, tracker's break to drink some strong Bedouin coffee laced with ample doses of cardamom. Sigalit Katz

by the thousands and served in Unit 300 as well as elite infantry and paratroop formations throughout the IDF.

Many outstanding and colorful Bedouin military personalities would emerge from this union—the most famous being Lt. Col. Amos Yarkoni. A native of the Hamazrib tribe, Yarkoni was a former anti-Jewish terrorist who, while on the run from the British, was befriended by Moshe Dayan and enlisted into the Jewish cause. He became a founding father of the IDF's reconnaissance strategy, commanding numerous elite units, including Sayeret Shaked, the Bedouin-inspired Southern Command recon force. During his thirty-plus years of service in the IDF, Yarkoni lost an arm, lost the use of a leg and an eye, and became one of the most decorated soldiers in IDF history. Other Bedouin officers and NCOs followed suit, earning an impressively high number of bravery medals in an army that sets extremely high standards for their issuance.

Although Bedouins have distinguished themselves as expert soldiers and border police, their inherent knowledge of the desert has been their claim to fame. They were the inspiration behind the creation of the Gashashim, or Trackers Unit, a force of Bedouins whose ability to read the desert sand was a natural wonder—and a military necessity. The Trackers Unit was formed in the aftermath of the 1967 War and was the original idea of Maj. Gen. Yehoshua Gavish, OC Southern Command. Although originally staffed by only ten Bedouins, the unit was formed to stop Palestinians from crossing the new and elongated border with Jordan. The Trackers Unit eventually expanded as tales of Bedouin heroism in the IDF spread throughout the thirty tribes of the Negev Desert and northern Galilee. In 1972, the Bedouin Sayeret Ha'Gmalim, or Camel Recon, was formed; the unit was charged with covertly following suspected terrorists in the Gaza Strip and seeking out PLO ammunition dumps amid the wilderness of the Sinai Desert. Its motto became, "The words *impassable terrain* are not in the Bedouin dictionary!"

The trackers' role is simple: observe and patrol a thinly sanded road along the border fences and interpret marks on the sand to determine if a terrorist, smuggler, or intelligence agent has crossed into Israel. After the intruder is detected the tracker is responsible for following the tracks and pursuing the infiltrator with "extreme prejudice." Every border patrol along Israel's vast frontiers is led by at least one Bedouin tracker. As one IDF officer proudly said: "A Bedouin tracker can determine more facts about the intentions of a terrorist from a footprint than weeks of intelligence work can ever hope to achieve. The Bedouins are Israel's human bloodhounds."

In this age of high-tech ground surveillance radars and electronic sensory devices safeguarding Israel's borders, it would appear as if the trackers' role would be obsolete. Nothing, however, could be further from reality. By judging the size and imprint of a footprint, an experienced tracker can ascertain the direction in which the terrorist has headed as well as determine the weight and load carried by the terrorist.

Although it is conceivable to train a Jewish soldier to learn the art of tracking, that instruction could never match the lifetime of practice that contributes to the tremendous proficiency of the

Bedouin trackers attempt to piece together the puzzle of mysterious marks in the desert as they follow a trail that, they fear, will lead to armed infiltrators from across the Egyptian frontier.

Bedouin. According to Sergeant Major Suleiman, a Bedouin NCO having almost twenty years of experience with the Golani Brigade: "To be a tracker, you have to be a shepherd or a herdsman, or at least the son of one. When a sheep or goat goes astray, you have to find it, and you do this by following footsteps!"

Bedouin trackers have been decisive in safeguarding Israel's frontiers from terrorist infiltration. For IDF units serving frontier duty, the Bedouins in their ranks also add the important elements of pride and tradition. At the end of each successful pursuit, for example, Bedouin trackers gather for a typical Bedouin celebration that marks the end to an eventful day in the field: a feast of lamb stew, followed by dozens of cups of strong Bedouin coffee laced with cardamom.

What separates the Bedouins from the other minorities serving the IDF is their perception of their military contribution as sacrosanct. The nomadic Bedouins have historically been at odds with the urban Palestinians, viewing their city-dwelling lifestyle with passionate disdain. During the 1967–70 War of Attrition, the IDF's Bedouins were instrumental in defeating PLO attempts to infiltrate hundreds of terrorists into the Jordan Valley. The wide-open desert spaces, mountainous terrain, and 50 degree Celsius heat made it a military campaign that was difficult for the IDF, but not for the Bedouins who volunteered for the opportunity to hunt down their Palestinian cousins. This racial animosity, in fact, is shared by Bedouins throughout the Arab world. When the Black September Jordanian Civil War erupted in 1970, King Hussein unleashed his own zealous Bedouin legions to eliminate once and for all the Palestinian terrorist presence in his kingdom. Encountering violence that would overshadow the later Sabra and Shatilla massacres, hundreds of Palestinian guerrillas opted to cross the Jordan River and escape into Israel rather than face the wrath of King Hussein's vengeful Bedouins. In an odd twist of fate, many of the Palestinian guerrillas who crossed the Jordan River to seek a kinder fate in Israel found themselves surrendering to Bedouins in IDF uniforms.

The trackers serving the IDF come from over thirty Bedouin tribes scattered throughout the Jewish State—from the sandy wasteland of the Negev Desert to the plush, rolling hills of Galilee. They have largely been an unheralded force whose enormous self-sacrifice has not been sufficiently appreciated by the Israeli public. In the past decade, however, the IDF has offered its Bedouin legions a unique symbol of its appreciation for over forty years of faithful service, with the creation of Sayeret Ha'Beduim, a truly segregated force of Bedouin soldiers, all trackers and paratrooper trained, whose job is to mount special defensive operations in southern Israel for Southern Command. For all purposes, it has replaced Sayeret Shaked as the first line of defense along Israel's southern tier.

Why Sayeret Ha'Beduim? Why now? For a brief period, the Israeli border with Egypt was the one quiet border area that was not surrounded by minefields and heavily armed patrols. It was known as the Peace Frontier. The only action that the IDF's Bedouin trackers encountered was stopping drug smugglers moving a lucrative hashish crop to and from Egypt or the odd backpack-toting

Four Bedouin trackers, all experienced terrorist hunters, confer along the Jordanian frontier after suspicious tracks that could belong to a Palestinian gunman are discovered.

traveler who got lost in the desert. Yet, in 1985, Palestinian terrorists based outside the territories, primarily Yasir Arafat's el-Fatah and Ahmed Jibril's PFLP-GC, attempted to seize headlines as well as disrupt the Egyptian-Israeli Peace Treaty by committing violent suicide attacks against southern Israel. Naturally, the terrorists based in Tunis and Damascus opted to attack from the Egyptian frontier, since it was not as meticulously secured as the Lebanese or Jordanian frontier. The Israeli border with Egypt was loosely defended and considered a physical statement of the precarious peace that existed between Jerusalem and Cairo. All that stood between the many heavily populated agricultural settlements in Israel's south and the determination of heavily armed terrorists were the Bedouin trackers. It was a task for which they were outgunned.

The notion for Sayeret Ha'Beduim came from Maj. Gen. Moshe Bar-Kochba, former OC Southern Command, who realized that the best means to form close bonds to the various Bedouin tribes of the south was the creation of their own conscript Sayeret. It would not simply be a force of trackers with reconnaissance wings, and it would not be a force of reconnaissance commandos who knew nothing of the desert. Instead, the unit would be a microcosm of the Bedouin experience in the IDF—a force of reconnaissance troopers who knew the desert like the back of their hand and patrolled the southern frontier in heavily armed jeeps. For unit pride, they have their own wings and wear the Giva'ati Brigade's purple beret. After all, as the saying goes in Sayeret Ha'Beduim, "If the Druze can have their own reconnaissance force, then so can we!"

It is midnight along the Egyptian-Israeli frontier, and First Lieutenant A'ataf, a Sayeret Ha'Beduim officer, has been hard at work for nearly 8 hours in difficult conditions—the desert is a hellish inferno by day and an arctic tomb at night. Standing upright in his jeep, First Lieutenant A'ataf peers through his field glasses to check for smugglers or armed intruders. In case a pursuit is necessary, his driver, Salim, and his vehicle can negotiate the hilly terrain with the dexterity of a camel and the speed of an Indy 500 race car. Should A'ataf need to engage the terrorists alone,

the jeep mounts a mighty 120mm mortar, and an FN MAG complete with thousands of rounds of 7.62mm ammunition is mounted to the dashboard over his seat. "Nothing will get by us to attack one of the nearby settlements," promises A'ataf. "Nothing!"

The patrol will last until sunrise, at 0600 hours. The three men in the jeep—A'ataf, Salim, and the mortar operator and communications NCO, Mustafa—are all suffering from red eyes, exhaustion, and the beginnings of frostbite. Although they are insulated from the winter's chill by wooly pullover sweaters and parkas, tonight is freezing. Thankfully, however, always one jeepborne unit has stoked the fires on the icy sands and is roasting a pot of strong Bedouin coffee laced with cardamom. This beverage is the fuel that fires these patrols, according to Abu Nizar, a senior NCO in Sayeret Ha'Beduim, and a coffee break allows the reconnaissance soldiers the opportunity to brief each other on movements in the desert.

A cordial esprit de corps permeates the ranks of Sayeret Ha'Beduim. Everyone is greeted with a hearty "A'halan Wa'Sahalan," no saluting takes place, and the soldiers treat one another as family—not as comrades-in-arms. This amiable atmosphere should in no way fool anyone into thinking that these soldiers are Bedouin Boy Scouts. According to one former Sayeret Tzanhanim officer now serving as an intelligence officer in Southern Command: "They can rough it up with the best of them. They are tremendous shots, they are snipers without having to use scopes and can race through the desert sands faster and more efficiently than any other Sayeret in the IDF—even those we are not supposed to talk about!"

Back in the field, First Lieutenant A'ataf continues his jeepborne patrol. At a spot somewhere on the course, something suspicious is noticed. It is an empty cigarette box from the Alia Cigarette Company in Arab East Jerusalem. Could a terrorist have dropped it en route to an attack, or did the winds bring it to this temporary resting spot? Nervously cocking his Glilon SAR, A'ataf dismounts his jeep and proceeds on foot, faithfully followed by his vehicle. No marks of a human presence are found, and the box is tossed in the jeep for proper disposal back at base. Tired and aching red eyes are rubbed a few times, and the patrol continues. Southern Israel will be safe this night.

Although it would appear that the marriage between Jew and "minority" Arab is a happy one, severe problems do exist. Even though, per capita, Druze, Circassian, and Bedouin towns and villages account for the greatest percentage of professional soldiers serving the IDF, their educational, economic, and social share of the Israeli "pie" is dismal. For Druze, Circassians, and Bedouins in IDF service, the neglect and indifference to their people is a bitter pill to swallow. Many minority soldiers consider themselves abandoned and attribute their situation to the racist sentiments of many Israelis. To exacerbate this situation, many of Israel's Arab citizens who don't see fit to serve the Jewish State view the minority soldiers as traitors and infidels—often subjecting the soldiers and their families to harassment and violence. Several years back, such humiliation came at the hands of other IDF soldiers. At a training base in the Jordan Rift, commandos of the Golani Infantry Brigade taunted a Druze unit with shouts such as, "Dirty Arabs," and, "You should be taken care of the way Arabs from Gaza are"; the verbal assaults led to an inevitable fistfight.

The work of minority units, especially Sayeret Ha'Druzim and Sayeret Ha'Beduim, has been so admired that many of the IDF's top brass have called for the opening up of the Air Force, Intelligence Corps, and all other branches of service to all the minorities as a reward for their contribution. Oddly enough, Druze, Circassian, and Bedouin leaders have all vehemently opposed such a move, fearing that assimilation into a predominately Jewish environment would lead to a demise of their own unique and proud cultures. As a result, the IDF's minority soldiers remain a contradiction of the norm: soldiers in an Israeli uniform wearing Arab headgear. No matter what their sacrifices have been, and no matter what debt the Jewish State owes them, the minorities will remain, by design and by choice, separate but equal entities. They are, according to Maj. Gen. Yitzhak Mordechai, OC Northern Command, "a bridge to peace and an example for us all!"

A proud father looks at his creation: Maj. Gen. Moshe Bar-Kochba, former OC Southern Command, inspects the first graduating class of Sayeret Ha'Beduim recon infantry soldiers as proud tribal chieftains look on.

Commandos from Sayeret Ha'Beduim enjoy a brief cup of Bedouin coffee in the Negev Desert during a patrol of the Egyptian frontier. Although a Bedouin reconnaissance force once secured the area on camelback, jeeps are now the order of the day.

119

Chapter 7

Sayerot Mat'kal, Ya'Ma'M, and Mista'aravim: The Counterterrorists

Because of the covert and top-secret nature of their work, and since most of the photographs of their operations, personnel, and equipment are classified and state secrets of the highest order, three Israeli elite counterterrorist forces must be covered in only a brief context. They are Sayeret Mat'kal, or General Staff Recon, an enigmatic and mysterious force; the Yechida Meyuchedet Le'Lochama Be'Terror (Ya'Ma'M), or Police Special Antiterrorist Unit, the National Police Border Guard's counterterrorist–hostage-rescue unit responsible for handling all terrorist incidents inside Israel; and the Mista'aravim, or Arabists, a two-front IDF antiterrorist unit that operates in the West Bank and Gaza Strip and whose soldiers masquerade as Arabs. Unfortunately, information on, and illustration of, these fascinating special forces is rarely released for publication.

Sayeret Mat'kal

The General Staff Recon Unit was founded in 1957 by an upstart intelligence officer named Avraham Arnan. Arnan believed in his heart that the IDF urgently required a force of intelligence-gathering commandos who could be despatched on top-secret missions into enemy lands and, to put it simply, execute the impossible missions. His vision came from bitter experience. In December 1954, three Sayeret Tzhanim NCOs and a Golani lieutenant were captured by Syrian soldiers atop the Golan Heights as they changed a battery on a listening device they had earlier affixed to Syrian telephone lines. Their seizure, and subsequent torture and imprisonment, prompted Arnan to petition the IDF General Staff and A'man to create the IDF's own force of rogue warriors that would be based on the example of Unit 101 and include the finest commandos from Sayeret Tzhanim; naturally, it was to be led by Lt. Meir Har-Zion. Har-Zion's injury a year later and other military preoccupations, like the 1956 War, delayed Arnan's ultimate vision, as did IDF bureaucracy and the General Staff's fear that this force would either be incapable of achieving spectacular feats behind

Sayeret Mat'kal commandos assist frightened, though relieved, ex-hostages from the Sabena Boeing 707 hijacked to Lod on May 8, 1972.

enemy lines and embroil the State of Israel in some type of conflagration or become too good for anyone's good and soon explode out of control.

In 1957, after resorting to small forms of extortion, bribery, and other methods of Byzantine business dealing, Arnan finally received his unit, and Sayeret Mat'kal was born. Initially, the unit was small—very small: it was rumored that the entire force could fit into the cargo hold of a Land Rover!

Major Arnan believed his unit should follow the example of the British SAS, and the motto Who Dares Wins even adorns the unit's mess to this day. To acclimate itself to enemy territory, the unit would learn to become its enemy, and Arnan despatched his warriors, who were primarily of European background, to the desert to learn how to become Arabs from Bedouin instructors; each commando would eventually adopt an Arabic nom de guerre beginning with the Arabic Abu, or Father of. For the most part, however, the unit was inactive. The General Staff was wary of providing it with operational assignments, and Major Arnan was busy recruiting.

Israeli soldiers couldn't just volunteer into the unit; Arnan had to observe them first in their parent unit and then offer them the opportunity to volunteer. The hapless soldiers would then be subjected to a series of grueling examinations,

In Tel Aviv on March 5, 1975, commandos inch their way closer to the Savoy Hotel, seized by seaborne Black September terrorists. The hotel was eventually destroyed by booby-trapped charges in the middle of the Sayeret Mat'kal rescue assault. IGPO

Dressed in Syrian-style lizard-pattern camouflage fatigues and meant to impersonate Idi Amin's entourage of Palestinian bodyguards, Sayeret Mat'kal commandos return from Entebbe—in Idi Amin's infamous black Mercedes—following the successful execution of Operation Thunderball, or Operation Yonatan, on July 4, 1976.

some of which were barbaric and cruel, to prove their worth as potential members of Sayeret Mat'kal.

Everything changed in 1959, however, when a conscript named Ehud Barak joined the unit. Sayeret Mat'kal and Israeli special operations would never be the same. Barak proved to be Meir Har-Zion's successor. Physically fit, innovative, highly intelligent, charismatic, and extremely courageous, he had a presence that would soon come to personify Sayeret Mat'kal; in fact, residents of his home Kibbutz "affectionately" referred to him

as a "lock-picking bastard" for his mischievous habits. Through his many operations behind enemy lines, Barak would become the most decorated soldier in Israeli history, would eventually command Sayeret Mat'kal, and would one day be the IDF chief of staff.

Between 1959 and 1967, Sayeret Mat'kal participated in several top-secret operations behind enemy lines—most of which remain classified. It *is* known, however, that the unit executed a highly successful intelligence-gathering mission in Syrian territory in August 1963.

Whatever the extent of their operations, the unit's members were excellent rogue warriors and intelligence gatherers: Israel's superb intelligence successes before and during the 1967 War are poignant evidence of their efforts and talents. Sayeret Mat'kal's role during the Six Day War is considered classified, although it is believed the unit saw extensive action on the Sinai front.

Sayeret Mat'kal revolutionized the IDF, even though it was a secretive force that very few IDF soldiers—including high-ranking officers—ever heard about. Its innovations were varied: they ranged from developing heliborne infiltration techniques to convincing Israel Military Industries to produce the 9mm Uzi submachine gun with a folding stock.

For a force of commandos considered to be the finest soldiers that the IDF could produce, designed by their mandate to perform extremely precarious intelligence-gathering missions behind enemy lines, the members of Sayeret Mat'kal would achieve fame not as soldier spies, but rather as counterterrorists. The 1967 War's aftermath would produce new warriors to the Middle East equation, the *international* terrorists, and only one group of soldiers could meet them on the field of battle: Sayeret Mat'kal. Between 1968 and 1992, Sayeret Mat'kal participated in some spectacular counterterrorist operations and produced some of Israel's most flamboyant and infamous soldiers. Some of Sayeret Mat'kal's infamous actions include the following:

During a fair in Ramat Gan, a sprawling Tel Aviv suburb, Ya'Ma'M antiterrorist commandos patrol the grounds as a preventative measure against a possible terrorist attack. Sigalit Katz

● Operation Gift, the December 27, 1968, heliborne raid into Beirut International Airport in which thirteen aircraft of Middle East Airlines—the Lebanese flag carrier—were destroyed in retaliation for Palestinian hijackings and terrorist attacks against El Al.

• Operation Mania, the July 20, 1969, raid conducted in conjunction with the naval commandos against the Egyptian Red Sea fortress of Green Island, a position considered by most sane military planners to be impregnable.

• Operation Isotope 1, the May 8–9, 1972, hostage rescue mission where commandos from Sayeret Mat'kal, led by unit commander Ehud Barak, masqueraded as airline mechanics in white coveralls and stormed a Sabena Belgian Airlines Boeing 707 hijacked to Lod Airport in Israel by Black September terrorists.

• Operation Crate 3, the June 21, 1972, Sayeret Mat'kal kidnapping of five Syrian intelligence officers, including several generals, who were conducting a terrorist-liaison tour of the Israeli border with Palestinian terrorists. The true objective of the raid, however, was to precipitate a prisoner swap with Syria, since Damascus was holding three Israeli airmen.

• Operation Spring of Youth, the April 9–10, 1973, foray deep into Beirut where Sayeret Mat'kal commandos, led by Ehud Barak, masqueraded as women, businessmen, and hippies and assassinated three of the top leaders of Black September in their West Beirut homes. One of the young Sayeret Mat'kal officers to play a significant role in the operation was Maj. Yonatan ("Yoni") Netanyahu.

• Operation Thunderball, the July 3–4, 1976, infamous IDF raid in which Sayeret Mat'kal, Sayeret Tzanhanim, and Sayeret Golani were flown to Entebbe, Uganda, to rescue 103 Israeli and Jewish hostages held by German and Palestinian terrorists and secured by Ugandan military units. Sayeret Mat'kal's job was to eliminate the terrorists and secure the hostages; the commandos' skill, courage, and ability to pull off the impossible entered international folklore. The lone Israeli fatality, Lt. Col. Yoni Netanyahu, Sayeret Mat'kal commander, became a symbol to the world of how Israeli special operations officers lead from the front and, sometimes, pay the ultimate price for their courageous means of command.

Although they were never confirmed by the IDF, foreign reports credit Sayeret Mat'kal with other spectacular operations, including the April 16, 1988, assassination of Abu Jihad, PLO deputy commander, in his Tunis home and the July 28, 1989, abduction of Sheikh Abdul Karim Obeid, Hizbollah's southern Lebanon commander, from his home in the heavily fortified village of Jibchit in a dazzling heliborne operation.

Yet, it has been many of Sayeret Mat'kal's counterterrorist operations *inside* Israel that have come to personify the very essence of the unit's existence. Its signature of being the only force that the Jewish State can rely upon to rescue its hostages adorns many incidents inside Israel, from assaulting the terrorist-held Savoy Hotel in Tel Aviv on March 5, 1975, to, according to foreign reports, killing a force of bus hijackers near the Gaza Strip on April 4, 1984. The most significant and controversial operation occurred on May 15, 1974, when three Palestinian terrorists from Nayif Hawatmeh's DFLP crossed the Israeli frontier from Lebanon

An antiterrorist policeman demonstrates firing his Galil sniper rifle during hostage rescue assault training at the Ya'Ma'M's home base somewhere in central Israel. Israel Military Industries

123

and seized a schoolhouse and over 100 junior high students in the town of Ma'alot. Fearing an Israeli assault, the terrorists placed explosive charges throughout the building. Faced with an impossible situation, the IDF OC Northern Command, Maj. Gen. Raful Eitan, ordered in commandos from Sayeret Mat'kal. But their attack failed. Their plan hinged on a sniper removing one of the terrorists, providing the remainder of the assault force with a 3-second window of opportunity to enter the building unnoticed. The sniper's lone shot hit the targeted terrorist but failed to kill him. Gun and

A Ya'Ma'M classified ad in the pages of the IDF's weekly newspaper offers employment to released officers and soldiers from the IDF's various elite forces. Sigalit Katz

grenade fire soon erupted. Before the commandos had a chance to liberate the hostages, the terrorists turned their guns on their hostages and then themselves. In all, twenty-two children were killed and over sixty wounded. The Ma'alot Massacre would change Israel forever.

Ya'Ma'M

The Ma'alot Massacre convinced many inside Israel's defense hierarchy that a special hostage-rescue force was required to deal with terrorist incidents inside Israel proper. In much the same way that the West German Border Police would create its elite GSG-9 antiterrorist commando force in the aftermath of the 1972 Munich Olympic Massacre, so, too, would the Israeli Police Border Guard create its own special antiterrorist force. It would be known by its Hebrew acronym Ya'Ma'M and would develop into the world's premier hostage-rescue force.

From its inception, in 1974–75, Yechida Meyuchedet Le'Milchama Be'Terror, or Ya'Ma'M, trained incessantly in the art of rescuing hostages, but for years, it never participated in a successful hostage-rescue operation. Although the unit did serve with great distinction as a commando entity in Lebanon during Operation Peace for Galilee, seizing and eliminating some of the PLO's most wanted men, no one ever gave it the chance to prove its worth. The opportunity to make a name for itself in the task for which it was mandated, to rescue hostages, finally came in the winter of 1988.

In the early morning hours of March 7, 1988, three heavily armed members of el-Fatah's Force 17 special operations unit crossed the Egyptian-Israeli border. Unlike the band that had crossed the same frontier a month earlier, these terrorists were the elite of what Abu Jihad could field, and, as such, they signified how much such an attack meant to Jihad. Their "professionalism" showed in the way they ruthlessly went about their task. They cut through the fence, and, at 0630, they commandeered a white Renault 4 on the mountain road in the southern Negev Desert. The efficient Israeli internal security apparatus went into full gear. The isolated desert Kibbutzim and Moshavim were notified of the terrorist infiltration through telephone and short wave, and their gates sealed shut. Air raid sirens ordered the women and children into the shelters and the men into defensive positions with weapons in hand. Throughout the Negev Desert, dozens of sleepy-eyed police officers rushed into their vehicles for tense patrols, and roadblocks supported by heavily armed police officers were set up at key intersections from the Egyptian frontier to the outskirts of Tel Aviv. As a colossal police pursuit of the white Renault 4 commenced in the beautiful sandy wilderness of southern Israel, a call went through from the National Police operations center in Jerusalem ordering the Border Guard antiterrorist commandos to be placed on a full alert.

By 0715 hours, the terrorists had reached their first roadblock at the Yerucham-Dimona Junction. It failed to stop them, as they swerved around the obstacles and sped on their way. A half-hour-long chase followed, with the police shooting unsuccessful bursts of gunfire at the terrorists' tires and having fire returned. IDF forces on maneuvers nearby joined in the fray, firing unsuccessfully upon the Renault as it passed by. Along the road to Dimona, the terrorists ditched their listing, bullet-riddled car and tried but failed to commandeer a semitrailer. They then set up a textbook guerrilla ambush, hoping to snare their next means of transportation before the Israelis arrived.

Moments later, an intercity bus carrying workers from their homes in Beersheba to the Nuclear Research Center in Dimona appeared. The driver managed to identify the three figures racing toward his Volvo bus as terrorists and screeched to a hasty stop. He opened his doors and ordered the passengers to escape, but eight women and one man were trapped on board when the three Palestinians assumed control of the vehicle. Seconds later, the vanguard of the police pursuit force reached the scene, as did Maj. Gen. Yitzhak Mordechai, OC Southern Command, and his advance command team. A stand-off ensued.

In the Renault, IDF officers found a rucksack full of grenades, which the terrorists had apparently forgotten, and the semitrailer's driver was questioned in order to gather some impromptu field intelligence. While the bus was gingerly surrounded by ad hoc response teams consisting of dozens of police officers and hastily summoned IDF soldiers, the district police commander, Haim Ben Oyen, commenced the negotiations in fluent Arabic, hoping to gain some time and an invaluable psychological insight.

Within minutes, the area had become the busiest location in Israel. Dozens in the Israeli defense community's who's who reached the scene. Helicopters flying overhead turned the thick desert morning air into a sandy cyclone, and the dust kicked up from the dozens of Army cars, trucks, and ambulances made visual command and control difficult. An elite IDF unit, believed to be from Sayeret Mat'kal, prepared a defensive perimeter surrounding the embattled bus and planned an assault. This unit was reinforced a while later by the rescue force from the Ya'Ma'M.

The terrorists holding the Beersheba-Dimona bus were well-trained professionals armed with numerous automatic weapons and grenades. Their determination to have a bloody firefight was expressed numerous times between 0900 and 1000 hours when they fired bursts of 7.62mm fire at the surrounding crowds and threw fragmentation grenades at encroaching IDF soldiers. Through the

On March 7, 1988, Ya'Ma'M commandos storm a bus seized by three el-Fatah Force 17 terrorists near Beersheba.

hails of gunfire, Ben Oyen attempted a sporadic dialogue with the three Palestinians. They demanded the release of Palestinian prisoners from Israeli jails and safe passage to a friendly Arab nation. Ben Oyen pleaded with the terrorists to stop the gunfire, but his anguished appeals for calm were rebuffed with the promise to throw a body out of the bus every 30 minutes.

The decision of when to act, always difficult to judge, was imposed when gunfire was heard from inside the bus at 1000 hours. Dissatisfied with the Israeli response to their demands, the terrorists opted to strengthen their position by killing a hostage in cold blood. As Chief of Staff Dan Shomron and OC Southern Command Mordechai—a man already quite intimate with such situations—retreated to a command post in a small sand hill meters away, the Ya'Ma'M was ordered to prepare its gear and its final assault plan.

For the Border Guard counterterrorist commandos, wearing bulletproof vests and carrying the ultracompact and deadly Mini-Uzi 9mm submachine gun, this was to be their moment of truth. The members of the hostage-rescue unit were keen to prove their worth. All veterans from the IDF's elite combat and reconnaissance units, those

volunteering into the Ya'Ma'M are trained in a brutally paced regimen of hand-to-hand combat, cold-weapon-killing, marksmanship, judo, Krav Maga (an Israeli-inspired form of intuitive martial arts), and split-second synchronized assaults on terrorist- and enemy-held targets. Each Ya'Ma'M "police officer" is trained to proficiency in every type of infantry weapon imaginable: from a K-Bar knife to a handgun, from an assault rifle to an RPG-7. Special emphasis is given to urban combat training, in both daytime and nighttime, and to eliminating terrorists in the first burst of gunfire so that hostages can be rescued unharmed. As a result, all members of a squad are expert in any task they might be called on to perform.

Given their background, the rescuers were not strangers to participation at the cutting edge of combat operations. They fully understood their profession's fatal vision. When the decision was issued ordering them into action, it was a moment of anxious fear each fighter would remember for years to come, especially for the Ya'Ma'M's commanding officer, Deputy Superintendent A.

At 1015 hours, after shots were once again heard inside the bus, the Ya'Ma'M exploded into action. Moments later, the three terrorists, wearing T-shirts with the word Palestine emblazoned across the chest, were killed. Just seconds prior to the rescue assault, however, the terrorists man-

At Nitzanim, Ya'Ma'M officers stand over the weapons and personnel tasked with carrying out a massacre on the Tel Aviv shore on May 30, 1990.

aged to kill two more hostages, adding a tragic end to a brilliant and decisive operation for the Border Guard commandos.

Much of the Ya'Ma'M's training is highly classified and involves all sorts of top-secret equipment; exotic weaponry, such as Mini-Uzi submachine guns fitted with laser sights and silencers, and stun grenades; and electronic and heat-sensory surveillance devices. Ya'Ma'M sharpshooters are considered the finest in Israel, and these antiterrorist police officers are all expert in the martial arts and varying degrees of cold-killing. A favorite training exercise is to pull up alongside a firing range in a speeding jeep, burst out of the vehicle, and engage the targets with guns ablaze. One aspect of the Ya'Ma'M that is not classified is that each Ya'Ma'M commando is an expert combat soldier. The Ya'Ma'M only accepts former IDF elite unit veterans, preferably officers or senior NCOs.

The Ya'Ma'M soldiers are an on-call force, on alert 24 hours a day, 365 days a year. They are always prepared to rush to any contingency and prevent any more massacres inside Israel.

Mista'aravim

On the night of June 21, 1991, the citizens of Israel were afforded a unique opportunity to view one of the nation's most secretive units in action. The Friday TV news showed filmed images of the Mista'aravim, a covert commando unit that masquerades as Arabs in order to neutralize key leaders of the Intifadah. It was the first time most Israelis had heard of this force. At first, the report showed three Arab men and one middle-aged Arab woman wearing traditional garb walking past a car and two motorists talking outside the market in Nablus. As the four individuals came close to the vehicle, they threw off their Arab costumes, produced 9mm Berettas and Mini-Uzi's from special holsters, and subdued the two suspects, throwing them into an awaiting vehicle. The four "Arabs" were members of the Mista'aravim, the special response force for dealing with sensitive terrorist targets in the occupied territories.

For years, news of two mysterious IDF reconnaissance paratrooper commando units operating in the territories had been filtering through the foreign media: Shimshon, or Samson, which oper-

ated in the Gaza Strip, and Duvdevan, or Cherry, which served in the West Bank of the Jordan River. Initially, when news of these two units first appeared, they were labeled as nothing more than assassins—heavily armed, cold-blooded killers who eliminated the leaders, or key individuals, of the Palestinian uprising. Yet, as the news coverage continued, viewers were offered a chance to see that the unit's primary weapon is surprise and disguise. The unit labored in presenting itself as Arabs in order to blend into the local communities. The commandos were seen donning Kefiyeh headdresses, Galabiya gowns, and fake moustaches and beards put on with vegetable glue; several even put on falsies and disguised themselves as women.

Lieutenant Colonel A., the Mista'aravim commander, explained: "We move around in the field, where our disguises are our principal weapons. We move about as masked youths, women, old men, and other locals. As long as we maintain our cover, we are safe. The moment we pull our guns, we must compromise our identities and go into immediate action. We try, at all costs, not to use force in the execution of our duties." Just in case, however, the Mista'aravim are expert marksmen. In the 1991 TV news report, they were seen running an obstacle course firing their Mini-Uzi submachine guns on the run. Of course, all the targets were hit. When they ran out of ammunition for their Mini-Uzis, the commandos removed 9mm Berettas from ankle holsters and pumped some close-quarter destruction into the center of their targets.

The Mista'aravim need to be expert shots. The terrorists don't play by any known rules. On March 5, 1992, the Mista'aravim suffered its first fatality when Sgt. Baruch Ben-Shimon, a commando from one of the Mista'aravim's Shimshon units, was killed in a gun battle with terrorists from the Popular Front in the Gaza Strip; the terrorist gunners, naturally, were immediately killed by Ben-Shimon's comrades-in-arms, who removed their Mini-Uzis from underneath their gowns and opened fire.

With the Intifadah entering its final and bloody stage, complete with the use of automatic weapons and explosives, the Mista'aravim will certainly become one of the IDF special forces' busiest units.

Index